Buffy the vampire slayer™

S+AKE Y⊕UR DES+INY

KEEP ME IN MIND

Buffy the Vampire Slayer™

Available from POCKET BOOKS

Buffy the Vampire Slayer™

STAKE YOUR DESTINY

KEEP ME IN MIND

Nancy Holder

**An original novel based on the hit television series
created by Joss Whedon**

POCKET
BOOKS

LONDON NEW YORK SYDNEY TORONTO

POCKET BOOKS

An imprint of Simon & Schuster
Africa House, 64–78 Kingsway, London WC2B 6AH

www.simonsays.co.uk

Printed and bound in Great Britain

First Edition   10 9 8 7 6 5 4 3 2 1

A CIP catalogue record for this book is available from the British Library

ISBN 1-4165-0241-6

In memory of John Ritter

Acknowledgments

Thanks to the following for helping me find my way: my agent, Howard Morhaim, and his assistant, Allison; my editor at Simon and Schuster, Patrick Price, and his colleague, Beth Bracken. At Fox, Debbie Olshan. At Mutant Enemy, the shiny Joss Whedon, and the staff, casts, and crews of *Buffy* and *Angel*. For tech and editorial support, *mahaho nui loa* to Wayne Holder. To Belle Holder, for reminding me that I am an A.G. Thank you to Liz Engstrom, Kym Toia, and Christie Holt. And thanks to the many, many others too numerous to name, who got me here and then helped me go there.

Dig a bit in the history of this place and you'll find there've been a steady stream of fairly odd occurrences. I believe this area is a center of mystical energy. Things gravitate toward it that you might not find elsewhere . . . like werewolves. Zombies. Succubi, incubi . . . everything you ever dreaded under your bed and told yourself couldn't be by the light of day.

The influx of the undead, the supernatural occurrences. It's been building for years and now . . . there's a reason why you're here, and there's a reason why it's now.

—Rupert Giles,
"Welcome to the Hellmouth"

Dear Buffy,

I find myself in the rather curious predicament of being forced to communicate with you in writing. By attempting to read the pages that follow, I've come under a spell that prevents my speaking to you of them directly. So please pay good attention to what I've written here.

I've been your Watcher for approximately a year and a half, and you are soon to celebrate your seventeenth birthday. We've had a number of rather remarkable adventures together, have we not? Defeating the Master ranks at the top, of course. Preventing Marcie Ross from carving Cordelia's face into a jack-o'-lantern was also rather good. And sparing me a violent death at the hands of that talent show demon as well, for that matter.

You've rescued Xander from his various demonic amours—Ampata and Miss French. And speaking of spawning, the dispatching of the Bezoar was extremely well done. Of course the destruction of Spike and Drusilla in the church fire is of great importance, perhaps even more significant than the destruction of the Master, though it's hard to judge . . . but I digress. And may I add that you and Kendra performed splendidly together. You were quite decent to her, as well, and I . . . I was quite proud of you, actually. One could go on . . . and on . . . but I'm sure I've lost your attention and you are now thinking about clothes.

Perhaps this will help you focus: You are about to embark on what may be the most crucial adventure of your slaying career thus far. Or rather, an entire collection of them. It's all in this magickal, wonderful-smelling book, which I discovered quite by accident while I was cataloging some obscure texts regarding television programming, of all things. I cannot decipher the literal text, as I have discovered that only a true slayer may look upon and comprehend the actual words. But it appears to be a blueprint of a series of quests all linked together; and if I understand it correctly, once you turn the pages, you will actually perform them—doing the actual work, as it were, not just reading about it. I've only got the bare bones of what is to come, but I must say it serves to underscore how very important it is that you continue to train and hone your skills. Lord knows, you are going to need them.

I'd like you to keep track of a few things. As we have discussed, your desire to live the "normal" life of an American teenager (as if any aspect of such an existence could be called normal, but yet again, I am straying from my topic) adds certain challenges to your role as the Slayer. We certainly don't need any more civilians learning about your slaying powers and all that entails. I know you find that problematic, and I realize that your relationship with your mother might go more smoothly if you could reveal your secret to her. It certainly would have eased tensions during that wretched Ted affair — sorry, "affair" is not quite the word I'm searching for.

So please, do be discreet around that young guitar player with the black fingernails. The one who got shot during Career Week — Oz. He's an enigmatic fellow, and I fear that he might see or hear something he ought not to. Likewise, Principal Snyder must not learn your secret under any circumstances. (I do wish Xander's "friends" had not devoured Principal Flutie; he was far more congenial and, frankly, easier to distract.)

On a more bizarre note, Xander and Cordelia have both become obsessed with closets. I've no idea what that means. And for my part, Miss Calendar has decided to give it another go, even after that bad run with Eyghon. Had it not been for Angel's ability to fight him . . . well, all I can say is that we are lucky to have a sympathetic vampire in our midst. Although I do wish the two of you could simply interact as colleagues, and not indulge in what you and your friends so mortifyingly term "smoochies." Ah, the California teen dialect — I shall never fully grasp it. Which, I hasten to add, is a point of pride with me.

As you proceed on these adventures, a word of caution is in order. As far as I can ascertain, you will have a terrible muddle on your hands if you simply go through the pages in consecutive order. That is to say, one, two, three, and so on, till you reach the end of the book.

Rather, start at the beginning, but follow the directions

at the bottom of each page. It appears that you'll have many such decisions, and that your decisions will guide you through a number of exciting quests with monsters and people whom you have come to love and/or loathe.

It does appear that things will come to a head in some sort of final battle—one assumes you will avert an apocalypse—so I do exhort you to choose your course wisely. It is up to you to read the enchanted pages that follow my note, and do as you think best.

And therefore, may I say, in closing . . .

. . . the world is doomed.

With all best wishes, your Watcher,

Rupert Giles

SLAYER ACTION:
Turn to page 1.

Y ou've been on patrol, with Angel, but it's near dawn and time to go home. The two of you two found more human bones and skin, so the monster you've been hunting is still at large.

You have promised, promised, promised to meet him again tonight. Same cemetery, same pair of kissable lips . . . mmmm.

You slip in through your window and flop fully clothed onto your bed. After a few precious z's and a shower, you slip on a peach slip dress and your kick suede boots with the high wooden heels. You load up your shoulder-strap purse with your makeup, a brush, a few nicely pointed stakes, a vial of holy water, and a pen for taking notes in class. Some coffee and a Krispy Kreme, and Mom's driving you to school.

"Can't wait for our mother-daughter date," she tells you with a big Joyce-Summers-size smile, smoothing back your hair. Which is unnerving because, well, look at how *she* wears *her* hair. "Where does all the time go?"

It goes toward fighting vampires, trying to pass school, and having some private time with Angel.

Ending any further mother-daughter quality time, the car pulls up to the palm-tree-lined Sunnydale High School. A quick kiss good-bye and you get out to find Cordelia Chase on the stairs in front of SHS, handing the last of a stack of pink flyers to Harmony, one of her Cordettes. They're invitations to the grand opening of Shoe Planet. You'll get 10 percent off if you flash the flyer. Queen C gets a discount for every utilized flyer, so she's happy to get one for you from her locker.

You shouldn't go to fetch that ticket to heaven. You should check in with Giles before first period. But . . . a discount? At a place called Shoe Planet? On a shopping trip with your mom, who has plastic?

SLAYER CHOICE:

Do you decide to . . .

\ go with Cordy? *If yes, turn to page 3.*

\ pass and move on? *If yes, turn to page 81.*

Greed wins over duty. You agree to go with Cordy to her locker. As she gets you a flyer, she glances in the mirror beneath her pic of Devon, the lead singer of Dingoes Ate My Baby, and discovers her lip liner is smudged.

"I have to work so hard to look this good," she murmurs. "I need a bigger mirror for this. I'm going to the girls' room. There's a few minutes before the bell rings. You know, you could use a fresh application, yourself."

You remember when she was the Queen of the Spring Fling last year, and how Marcie Ross nearly disfigured her for life. That was the first time you almost bonded with Cordelia—except you didn't.

A sudden wave of nausea hits you. Cordelia, of course, doesn't notice. You follow her to the girls' bathroom, feeling very dizzy and disoriented. Is there something going around? If so, you've caught it.

As you enter the bathroom, all the other girls are leaving—the next bell's about to ring, so it's just the two of you. Cordelia goes to the mirror; you go into a stall and shut the door . . .

. . . and then you hear her scream!

You fly out of your stall just in time to see her beautiful Steve Maddens dangling from an empty square of ceiling as she's yanked upward . . . and hear the maniacal, cackling laughter of the invisible, insane, Cordelia-hating Marcie Ross!

But those guys in black suits took Marcie away last year, after I stopped her from doing anti–plastic surgery on Cordy's face!

Thinking's for later. Adjusting your purse with its all-important Slayer accessories, you prepare to leap into the ceiling to go after them.

Just then, the girls' room door swings open, and Principal Snyder is staring right at you! "Are you screaming?" he demands. He sniffs the air. "And smoking in here *again*?"

Okay, Buffy. Let's see how quick you are today! Explain to Principal Snyder what is going on.

SLAYER CHOICE:

Do you decide to . . .

\ try the truth? *If yes, turn to page 5.*

\ offer a rat-based excuse for a rat-faced principal?
If yes, turn to page 10.

"**U**mm . . . I-I," you stammer. "No smoking. Ever. I have never smoked. But she—but I—oh, just forget it!'

You bend your knees, preparing to leap up. You can't really go all Slayer with him here, though. He needs to be gone!

Snyder taps you on the shoulder and says, "Excuse me? *'Forget it'?* I don't think so."

He lifts his hand in the air and snaps his fingers. A burly security guard steps up behind him, blocking the open door. He looks very mean. He also looks like he has a walkie-talkie to call other security guards. You could take him in an instant, but you doubt you could do so without causing a scene and revealing that you are the Slayer. You figure the quicker you cooperate, the quicker you can save Cordy.

"Let's go," Snyder says to you.

"But, I—" You glance uneasily at the ceiling.

"*Now,* Miss Summers," Snyder says once more with feeling.

"I really don't feel well," you plead. "I-I need to—"

"You need to come with me now, or you will be spending the entire day in detention—do you understand?"

"All right," you mutter, defeated.

A temporary condition, you remind yourself.

As you are walking down the hall, the security guard's walkie-talkie starts crackling with the Roger-10-4's. The guard listens for a minute and says, "Copy that."

Then he informs Principal Snyder, "Girl got stuck

in the ceiling. Cordelia somebody. She's okay now. A little shaken up, though. Wants to see her therapist."

Snyder shakes his head. "These kids. They're the worst part of my job."

"Cordelia . . . that's what I was trying—," you begin.

"No speaking," he orders you. "Walking. No talking. And, by the way, I'm going to be keeping my eye on you this school year. If I ever find you anywhere you're not supposed to be, I will happily expel you. I will be checking your classes. I will be talking to your teachers. I won't be talking to that foreign librarian, because he's a useless individual who should go back to Europe."

"He's not—" Why are you even arguing with him?

"No talking," he snaps. "None."

Grrr. Argh.

It's pretty clear that you'll have to solve the mystery of Marcie Ross later.

SLAYER ACTION:
Turn to page 7.

"**M**iss Summers," Principal Snyder says, his sour smile the very soul of smugness—the only soul Snyder has, you're willing to guess. "So nice to see you in my office. You can't imagine how it lifts my spirits."

As you face him, you so wish that Xander's ex–hyena friends had not devoured Principal Flutie.

"Just tell me what I'm in for," you grumble. Then, mustering every ounce of willpower in your entire body, you add, "Please."

"From now on, each and every morning of your school day will begin with some time together," he exults. "Before first period. In my office. For the rest of the school year, you will read your textbooks for an entire hour while I sit in my chair and gloat. For today, you'll spend first period with me." He gestures to a folding chair in the corner. "Sit, Miss Summers. And stay."

"I really can't—," you argue.

"Oh, you really can. And for every minute that you *don't* open your books and read, you will spend an additional *ten* with me *after* school every single day."

Gulp. After school? Make Giles wait? Make the Bronze wait? Make Angel wait? Make those of the bad wait? "All right," you say.

You open your health book and begin to read.

SLAYER ACTION:
Turn to page 8.

Let the reading begin.

Cutaway of a runny nose.

"Mucus, a slimy substance composed of salts suspended in water . . ."

Tick, tock, tick, tock . . . your eyes grow heavy.

". . . a miracle coating that prevents digestive acid from devouring the human stomach . . ."

You yawn.

"Milk encourages the production of mucus. . . ."

Tick, tock, tick, tock . . . Is that a split end?

"This slippery substance coats various organs. . . ."

Tick, tock, tick, tock . . . And a hangnail?

Tick, tock, tick, tock . . . You yawn.

SLAYER ACTION:

If you're in Snyder's office, turn to page 9.

*If you're doing the sneaky book cover research,
turn to page 147.*

Tick, tock, tick, tock.

What is with all this mucus?

Tick, tock, tick, tock . . .

You have more important things to do besides read about mucus!

The bell rings.

Snyder smiles. "See you tomorrow morning," he sneers at you. "Bright and early."

Face it, Slayer. You gotta be a little more resourceful. Pay attention and acquire the knowledge! You have much to learn.

THE END

"**S**ee, here's the thing," you blurt out. "There's a . . . there's a rat in the ceiling, so . . . so I'm going to go get it."

"What?" he asks incredulously. "If you think for a minute that I don't know you're up to something—"

Then someone taps him on the shoulder with short, black fingernails. It's Oz, that guy who likes Willow!

"Principal Snyder?" he says. "There's an electrical fire in the music room. Sorry—"

"What were you doing in the music room?" Snyder shouts.

"Playing music," Oz replies calmly.

"That's just wrong!" Snyder bellows. "You students, always using things and creating chaos!"

Snyder pushes past him and races out the door.

Oz looks at you. You look at Oz.

Does he know I'm the Slayer? you wonder. *Did Willow maybe share?*

He gives you a little wave and disappears back out the door.

No time to wonder if your secret—which isn't all that secret—is still the secret that it was. Or should have been.

But hey, good lie! Lie that worked! With the coast cleared, you clamber up into the ceiling.

There's a dim light from somewhere. You're in an air-conditioning duct and, ewww, it is *mucho* gross up here. Lots of trash and rat droppings—so you weren't lying to Snyder, exactly.

There's a path cleared through the gunk that you can follow—Marcie's gotta be dragging Cordelia, which means two things: (1) She drugged her again, and (2) she's going to get tired.

Tired a lot faster than you're gonna get tired.

As you hurry to catch up, you remember how bad you felt for Marcie last spring. She went all crazy and invisible because she was ignored. At the time, you wished you could have done something more for her besides just stopping her. But you couldn't. Maybe this could be some kind of second chance. . . .

You come to a fork in the tunnel. Left and right look equally cleared of debris, meaning Marcie could have gone either way. Which way to go?

SLAYER CHOICE:

Do you decide to . . .

\ go right? *If yes, turn to page 12.*

\ go left? *If yes, turn to page 18.*

Yₒₒ go right. In the dim light, you see Cordelia about ten feet directly ahead of you. She looks like she's lying on an invisible moving slant board, which means Marcie has probably hooked her arms under Cordy's arms and clasped them across Cordelia's chest. Cordy's head is lolling forward, and she is unconscious. There may even be some drool. . . .

You crawl forward, and suddenly Cordelia drops to the ground. You're glad she's unconscious, because if she knew what she was lying in, she would be screaming at the top of her lungs. And you know from experience that Cordelia has a real set of lungs on her.

Despite your desire to race after Marcie, you bend down and make sure she's breathing.

Her eyes flutter open, and she says, "Where am I?" Her eyes widen and dart left and right. "Am I lying in rat poop?"

"Um, a shower would be good," you say evasively. "But don't wig, okay? If you start screaming, I won't be able to go after Marcie."

"Marcie? Marcie Ross is back?" Her voice is shrill.

"Cordelia, *please,*" you beg.

Then, as you prepare to take off after Marcie, Cordelia grabs your calf and cries, "You can't leave me here!"

"The bathroom is back that way," you tell her.

But she is freaking out. "No, no, Buffy! I've been so traumatized!" Her voice is rising ever higher. "My hair! Oh my God! There is rat poop in my hair! Oh my *God*!"

What do you do? This is part of the gig you haven't yet figured out. Cordy's not exactly your friend, but she's upset. And you do not need civilians getting in your way—which may happen if you leave Cordy to fend for herself. She's totally lost it and she may want to share really, really badly.

SLAYER CHOICE:

Do you decide to . . .

❚ stop chasing Marcie and help Cordelia pick up the pieces of her shattered existence? *If yes, turn to page 14.*

❚ leave Cordy there and chase after Macie? *If yes, turn to page 18.*

Y ou want to say, "I'm the Slayer, not a high school counselor," but you only sigh.

Cordelia wipes her eyes. "Please, Buffy, take me back to the bathroom. I can't go anywhere looking like this. Just don't let anyone see me before I can reapply my makeup. . . ."

SLAYER CH⊕ICE:

Do you decide to . . .

\ return Cordelia to the bathroom? *If yes, turn to page 15.*

\ say, "Sorry Cordelia, but I have to chase after Marcie"? *If yes, turn to page 18.*

\ say, "Sorry, Cordelia, but I'm actually going to try to snag the end of first period so I don't have detention for the rest of my life, and therefore, I won't be able to go after Marcie"? *If yes, turn to page 20.*

"**O**kay, you win," you tell Cordelia as you help her down from the ceiling. You start to walk back toward the bathroom, but she whirls around to face you.

"No way!" she cries. "Not *that* bathroom! I'll never go in there again!" As you begin to protest, she says, "Please, Buffy. I've been abducted twice out of there! A girl can only take so much!"

Marcie Ross is out there—*up* there—and you know she is more dangerous than smudged makeup. So the sooner you get Cordelia taken care of, the better.

You hurry her down the main hall, looking left and right for Snyder. You know trying to explain the situation to him will land you in his office, so it's best to avoid him.

The coast appears to be clear, so you mutter, "Let's go."

"You can be so nice," Cordelia says. "It might be fun to be, you know, actual friends, except it wouldn't, because you're just so weird."

You glance at her; she whimpers, shielding her face from your gaze. She continues, "Have you always been weird, or did becoming the Slayer do it to you? It's so unfair. I mean, you have so many strikes against you. Divorced parents, getting booted out of your school in L.A. . . ."

You're touched. This is a deep conversation you're having, and with Cordelia of all people. It's more like Willow-in-jammies sleepover talk, and you wonder if maybe you have misjudged Cordelia.

". . . and then you wind up here, and make friends with the two most total losers in the entire school," Cordelia goes on. She gives you a look. "I tried to warn you, remember?" She wags her finger. "So much tragedy and heartbreak could have been prevented if only you'd hooked up with me and mine."

She shrugs her shoulders. "Oh well, that's ancient history. You blew it, and now you're a social pariah. Just like Marcie Ross." She looks at you sadly. "Thank God you didn't become invisible. Although, I suppose that might be useful for a vampire slayer."

At that very moment, Oz, the guitarist, steps into the hall. You hiss at Cordelia to be quiet, but she doesn't notice.

"I mean, you could sneak up on your enemies and, like, kill them. . . ."

"Whoa, harsh," Oz says by way of greeting.

My hair! Cordelia shrieks, rushing off in the opposite direction.

Oz looks at you. You look at Oz.

"Bad-hair day?" he asks.

You nod, then take off after Cordelia.

As Cordelia races back down the hall, you see the door to the home ec room burst open. "Cordelia!" you shout. "Look out!"

But it's too late. She's tackled by an invisible force that throws her to the ground. Something shiny flashes in the light. It's a scalpel, arcing into the air and slicing down toward Cordelia's neck.

You slide toward Cordelia, just in time to see the

scalpel change direction. Its sharp, pointy end is aimed at you.

You don't have time to react, but in the time-honored tradition of people facing their deaths, your entire life flashes before your eyes—or at least your entire morning does. You have a chance to realize that when you decided to snag a flyer for a discount on shoes instead of check in with Giles, you set into motion a tragic chain reaction of events that led you to this moment.

I wish I could do it over, you think.

Right before the scalpel pierces your jugular.

Cordelia starts shrieking, and footsteps clatter toward you. You look up to see your fellow students racing toward you. You see your friends—Willow and Xander. You see Oz. You see Giles.

But the last person on the planet you look upon before you die is Principal Snyder.

And that is too tragic for words.

THE END

Y ou're on the prowl! You're looking for a trail, for maybe a flute, or a nest like Marcie had last time. You remember her so vividly. Of course, before she turned invisible and evil, you wrote "Have a nice summer" in her yearbook just like everybody else did. That's the kiss of social death.

You go left, and then you collapse headfirst into open space! Down you fall, down, down, down, just like Alice in the rabbit hole, and you brace yourself for the big crash!

SLAYER ACTION:
Turn to page 19.

CRASH!

SLAYER ACTION:
Turn to page 23.

Y ou slip into class just as Ms. Kalosh, your health teacher, announces, "Okay, now that I'm finished lecturing on the mucus system, we're going to have a pop quiz. Everyone have a pencil?"

"How about a tissue?" Xander jibes. He smiles at you. "Hey, Buffy."

"Hey." You smile back weakly. Despite your best intentions, you do not have the knowledge. Sighing, you pull out a number two pencil and hope for the best.

"Buena suerte," Willow tells you. She's been in a Spanish kind of mood lately. You know that *buena suerte* means "good luck."

Only . . . you don't seem to have much.

You're done in no time, because you only knew a few answers. Salts, secretions, slime. Attention span, meet Buffy. Ms. Kalosh picks up your test, shakes her head, and begins to write you a hall pass.

"Principal Snyder told me that if you flunked this quiz, I was supposed to send you straight to his office," she informs you. At least she sounds sorry about it.

She hands you the pass. Then she frowns at you and says, "Are you feeling all right?"

"Not really," you mutter.

"Hmmm. There's a stomach virus going around." She picks up her blank pad of hall passes. "Do you want to go to the nurse's office first?"

You consider: Going anywhere, even hell, is preferable to Snyder's office. You think about resuming the important mission of the Slayage, but Snyder's going to be watching you. And you really don't feel good. Maybe a quick detour to see the nurse would be best.

On the other hand, Principal Snyder is a relentless little weasel who really has it in for you. Keep him waiting, watch him froth. Things might go easier for you if you just show.

SLAYER CHOICE:

Do you decide to . . .

❧ go to Snyder's office? *If yes, turn to page 7.*

❧ go to the nurse's office? *If yes, turn to page 22.*

Y ou decide to go to the nurse's office, a very small cubicle with walls covered with colorful posters about VD, drugs, and teen pregnancy. There is, however, no information on mucus. Seated at a desk behind a foot-high pile of charts, the nurse, Ms. Caulfield, looks up at you and says, "What's wrong with you?"

It takes an act of will to not respond, "Isn't that what you're supposed to find out?" However, your nausea has passed.

"Sit down. I want to take your temperature," she announces. She rises from her desk and turns around to get the ear thermometer off the shelf of medical instruments.

You sit down on the other side of the desk and cross your legs. Your knee brushes against something round and hard. Curious, you lean down to investigate.

Attached to the overhanging portion of the desk is one of Miss French's giant praying mantis eggs!

Without thinking, you make a fist and execute a totally righteous uppercut at the direct center of the crusty shell. Yes! You smash it to smithereens!

Unfortunately, you rip the desk apart as well.

Which can only mean . . .

SLAYER ACTION:
Turn to page 7.

Y ou're stunned for a few seconds, but yay, Super-Slayer healing powers. So you get back up again, just like in that infectious song by Chumbawamba, and . . . you're hit with another stomach-lurching wave of dizziness!

SLAYER ACTION:
Turn to page 24.

Y ou have managed to fall from the air-conditioning duct through the ceiling and down into the basement of Sunnydale High. Given how bizarre your school is, that doesn't surprise you too much.

Then you hear a low chuckle and a voice with a Southern accent that says, "Rise and shine, Slayer! We're here to fight to the death!"

And that surprises you a lot.

You blink, only to see the evil Texas vampire Tector Gorch standing on top of a hill of smelly mud or something worse, about ten feet away. But the Mother Bezoar, who infected SHS with her mind-controlling eggs, ate Tector Gorch just last week!

Yeah, and I was actually kinda pissed off that I didn't get to do it, you think as you leap to your feet. It's tempting to stay and slay . . . but your priority is the Marcie Ross situation. So you say, "Sorry. You're gonna have to take a number for your own private Alamo."

You turn away from him . . . to find your way blocked by his brother, Lyle! And you hear Tector jump off the hill and head for you!

SLAYER ACTION:
Turn to page 25.

Strategy time, Slayer! What has Giles taught you? Don't remember? No? Because you've put playing ahead of slaying? You make out with Angel during patrol, and you blow off training to hang with your friends at the Bronze?

SLAYER CHOICE:

Do you remember . . .

❚ what Giles taught you the night you killed the vampire that was wearing a ring from the order of Aurelius? *If yes, turn to page 26.*

❚ an interesting little fact about Emily Dickinson that Owen Thurman told you when the two of you were alone? *If yes, turn to page 27.*

❚ an interesting fact about your date night with Owen—something Giles gave you in case of the apocalypse? *If yes, turn to page 28.*

❚ nothing except the fact that you have a flyer for a discount at Shoe Planet, and you can't get blood out of suede? *If yes, turn to page 29.*

"*Plunge and move on.*"

He told you that in the cemetery. Get the job done. And he said your technique was all wrong too! Well, you'll show him!

"Hi," you say to Lyle. Then you drop, tuck, and roll. Tector's momentum slams him smack into his brother, and they both fall to the dirt in a tangle of arms, legs, and swear words!

You whip out a stake from your purse as you leap back up. You race over to them. You're looking for that little piece of heaven called the chest.

There's one now, covered in a filthy white T-shirt!

SLAYER ACTION:
Turn to page 30.

"**D**id you know that you can sing any poem by Emily Dickinson to the tune of 'Yellow Rose of Texas'?" you ask.

SLAYER ACTION:

If you're with the Gorch brothers,
turn to page 159.

If you're with Spike, turn to page 158.

"*If the Apocalypse comes, beep me.*"

So you told your Watcher, when he gave you a pager to take on your date with Owen. It did not work so well. Giles was nearly cremated, and Owen was almost killed.

Raising your brows in all innocence, you say to Lyle, "Oh hey, is that your beeper going off?"

He looks down, says, "Huh?" at the same time that Tector shouts, "It's a trick, you idjut! We don't *have* pagers!"

He charges!

Too late! In that moment of distraction, you whip out a stake and dust Lyle. Then you whirl and around use the same stake on Tector!

SLAYER ACTION:
Turn to page 30.

*N*ew shoes, Visa card, you remind yourself mournfully as you prepare to commit the final sacrifice. *And also, thank God for cheerleading.*

You look left, then right, as the two vampire brothers rush you. You can smell their stinky vampire breath, sweat, and beer. Lots of beer. Beer is bad.

Then you bend your knees and leap *not too high* into the air in a really fabulous side-split that surely would have landed you a better spot on the cheerleading team than first alternate if you had managed it at tryouts.

With perfect timing, your nice, long, *wooden* heels connect with the chests of the Gorch brothers!

SLAYER ACTION:
Turn to page 30.

*W*hoooooooosh!

It's a two-fer!

A double dust!

A double demon dust!

A double demon death dust of chocolaty deathness!

SLAYER ACTION:
Turn to page 31.

It is *so* beyond time to go see Giles.

You go to the library. As you swing through the double doors, Giles appears from his office with an enormous, dusty book in his arms.

"Hey, Giles. Something extremely weird just happened."

He raises his brows. "Oh, good Lord. You did your homework?" he asks.

"That is so not funny," you drawl. "But neither is this." You tell him.

"Wh-what? That's impossible." Giles sets the book down on the gleaming wood study table. Dust lifts from the heavy tome.

"And yet."

SLAYER ACTION:

If you're telling Giles about Marcie Ross,
turn to page 32.

If this is after the "death" of the person you
are closest to in this world,
turn to page 144.

Then Xander walks in with Cordelia, who is crying. "Did you hear?" she asks shrilly. "After you abandoned me, Harmony fell down the stairs and broke stuff! That's what Marcie did the first time she was here! She started picking off all my friends to get to me! It's all about me!"

"Right," Xander says, nodding. "It always is. By the way," he says to you and Giles, "speaking of Cordelia, Harmony has been taken to the hospital. She may require surgery."

"See how vicious she is?" Cordelia continues. "Oh, my God! I swear, I'll never get out of therapy, the way things are going around here! Buffy, you have to do something. I cannot handle this again!"

"No joy here, either," you say. You look at Giles. "Snyder is following me everywhere. It's going to be hard to look for her during school."

"Well, the day will be over eventually. Perhaps she will withdraw now that she's created some mayhem," Giles says reasonably. "She may feel the need to hide out, as it were. To refrain from doing anything else that calls attention to her presence."

"Unless she blows up the school!" Cordelia cries.

"What about the Gorches?" you ask. "Giles, Tector Gorch was devoured by the Bezoar. I saw it! I was there!"

"I was there too!" Cordelia cries. "Only, I was under mind control at the time, so I didn't actually process that brutal, wrenching death, but I'm sure it's lodged somewhere in my subconscious, and I'll be dealing with post-traumatic stress disorder for the rest of my life!"

"Easy, easy," Xander says to her.

"Oh, God!" She touches her face. "Is my eye makeup running?"

"Like the bulls at Pamplona," Xander assures her.

"No!" She presses her hands to her forehead. "Xander, will you—"she searches for words—"will you escort me to the bathroom so I can make myself look presentable? Buffy wouldn't do it."

"Hey, Slayer, not security service," you protest. "Or wait. Is that the same thing? Not makeup artist," you amend.

"Of course I will," Xander says to Cordelia. "And maybe we can find a nice closet on the way."

A closet? Do you get the weirdness of them?

"Oh!" Cordelia replies. Her eyes fill with what strangely looks like hope. "A closet . . ."

Xander smiles at her. "Yes. A nice, life-affirming closet. A closet where there are no monsters. Or mirrors. Or even, things to see. Just . . . darkness."

"And, preferably, silence," she says, smiling back. "Nothing to hear. No talking."

He pantomimes zipping his mouth and throwing away the key. Then they both chuckle.

They leave, and you say, half to yourself, half to Giles, "What was that all about?"

But Giles is of the Watcherness as he paces, pushing up his glasses. "You'll be patrolling the school tonight, of course," he says. "And I'll start researching this as soon as possible. The Gorches. And Marcie Ross. I'll make some calls. . . ."

Wait. Patrolling?

What about other things? Like smoochies, and buying new sandals and body glitter to wear during the having of smoochies?

You have a solemn duty. You are the Chosen One. The one girl in all the world who's supposed to risk her life night after night battling the forces of darkness. You are all that stands between the rest of the world and evil.

Not having enough shoes is evil, you think dismally.

Not seeing Angel is even eviler.

So . . . what are you going to do? You already know, don't you? You've told Angel you'll meet him in the cemetery. You are sixteen, and your boyfriend is a hottie. And you are in love.

Let's think this through. You figure Marcie will stay close to SHS to wreak her vengeance. And there won't be anyone here tonight. So . . . no problem if you don't patrol the school tonight.

There might be a night watchman, though. Would Marcie do anything to a grown-up?

Maybe even Snyder?

Meanwhile, Giles is on the phone. He says, "Yes, I'll hold." Then he looks over his shoulder and says, "You should go to your classes. If I hear anything, I'll contact you later, all right? I've got some texts at home. I'll need to go through them."

He's going into that special part of his brain that is Ponderous Land. You give him a nod that could mean . . . well, it means, good-bye, okay? That's all it means. It does not mean that you are telling him you will patrol.

SLAYER CHOICE:

Do you decide to . . .

❙ blow off patrolling the school and meet Angel in the cemetery after sunset? *If yes, turn to page 36.*

❙ blow off patrol and go to Shoe Planet with your mom? *If yes, turn to page 45.*

❙ patrol the school? *If yes, turn to page 55.*

Oh, Slayer. No, no, no.

When you were fifteen, maybe.

But the sixteen-year-old Slayer that you are now would *never, ever* blow off patrol when there was a real danger lurking in the shadows.

Let's rephrase that.

There is always a real danger lurking in the shadows. You live on the Hellmouth. Its evil vibe draws monsters and demons the way those electric bug-zappers draw pests. Except that bug-zappers *kill* the pests that are drawn to them. The Hellmouth seems to give your brand of pests a big shiny happy.

Marcie is back, and she has already hurt Harmony. Probably. And she tried to kidnap Cordelia again. Definitely.

So you have to patrol. You really do.

Lift that chin! Square those shoulders!

Yay, Buffy! You're doing the right thing!

Which is to trot down all the hallways—okay, run; duck into the caf, zoom up to the attic, and race down to the basement. Rattle some doorknobs, which are locked, and peer sideways at the frosted-glass panes in some classroom windows. Nothing is moving behind them.

Then you smile to yourself and say, "I have patrolled. I am good Buffy."

Okay, you've now . . . patrolled. It is off the list of to do. So . . . to the cemetery? All you have to do is make a quick call to your mom and say, "I'm so sorry, I have to study," which is not a lie. You do have to study. That doesn't mean you plan to do it right now.

Or . . . knowing that Mr. Cemetery has a very late curfew—actually, a very early one, ha-ha—you can keep that date with your mom and still see Angel. Yay, shopping! Yay, *smoochies* and shopping!"

So . . . who ya gonna call?

SLAYER CHOICE:

Do you decide to . . .

❚ call your mom and tell her that you're studying the Civil War with Willow? *If yes, turn to page 38.*

❚ keep your pre-date date (or is it a date? Are you and Angel dating?) with your mom (which can involve Shoe Planet!)? *If yes, turn to page 38.*

Stop.

Be honest.

Think this through. Marcie Ross has to be around here somewhere. You just haven't found her yet.

You weren't patrolling.

You were just going through the motions.

A glance here, a rattled doorknob there . . .

"I was not," you protest, even though your cheeks feel hot and you are feeling a little guilty. But hey, you *did* look. You covered the entire school! Well, except for the teachers' lounge. That place is deeply scary.

So . . . what are you in the mood for?

SLAYER CHOICE:

Do you decide . . .

\ Angel? *If yes, turn to page 39.*

\ shoes? *If yes, turn to page 45.*

\ real patrolling? *If yes, turn to page 55.*

Y ou hurry to the cemetery. Mist is rising from the ground, and the trees are scattering leaves in the wind . . . giving their branches an anorexic and basically skeletal look, but hey, nature. Night, stars, moon. It's all good.

And Angel is there, looking as lunchable as the One with the Angelic Face should look. Black pants, black shirt, black jacket. He holds out his arms, and you are so there. His lips press against yours, and you are so in love . . . and so glad you didn't stake him when you had the chance.

You almost did. His old—really old—skanky ho vampire girlfriend, Darla, bit your mom and then tried to pin the blame on Angel. You had just discovered he was a vampire—he vamped the first time you kissed, 'cuz of the passion—and later, when you got home from studying with Willow, you saw him bent over your mom. Her throat was torn and bleeding, and he was all vamped out. You thought the worst. . . . You could have killed him then.

But thank goodness you hesitated. Or rather, threw him out the window. You could never, ever kill Angel. And you will never have to. Because yes, he is a vampire, and yes, you are the Slayer. But he is the only vampire in all the world with a soul. Therefore, good.

And he is your soul mate.

Or so *you* think. You're not sure what Angel thinks. He's had so many girlfriends. You're only sixteen. Back in L.A., you were dateworthy—until the slaying started . . . but you've never dated an older man . . . a much older man . . . okay, a guy who's had a bicentennial. . . .

"Something's wrong," Angel says, pulling away and gazing hard at you. "What happened?"

"Nothing," you say, but he's not buying it.

You tell him all about it, and he shakes his head. "Marcie Ross, I can understand. She probably came back for vengeance. I've been there."

"But the Gorches . . . Angel, there should only be one Gorch. I saw two." You hold up two fingers. The ring on your forefinger sparkles in the moonlight. What would it be like to have Angel slip a ring on your finger?

You are being so immature.

So in love . . .

"The Gorches." He nods. "Tector was destroyed? You actually saw him dust?"

"Did see. Did dust. He was gone."

Angel frowns. "That doesn't happen. Once someone is dust, they can never come back," he says.

That gives you a wiggins. You start to feel more uncomfortable with all the death-thinking and the way the conversation is going.

"You could have been killed," Angel adds, as if he's picking up on that dreary conversation thread as well.

"But I wasn't," you point out. "I'm here. With you."

"What would I do . . . ?" Angel murmurs, then he shakes his head. "Never mind," he says.

"If I died?" you persist. "What would you do if I died?"

He pales. Wait. He's already pale. He . . . looks broody. Wait, he always looks broody. . . .

"Yes," he says softly. "What would I do?"

"Gee, maybe you would look pale and brood?" You're trying to be witty. But you can tell that, for Angel, the mood is blown. It kind of is for you, too. All this death-in-the-air is creeping you out. It seems that Angel really wants to talk about it. You . . . not so much.

So what do you do? Do you continue the discussion, or bottle it up and try to distract Angel? Can you discuss mortality, your future together, and all kinds of other scary and potentially depressing subjects?

SLAYER CH⊕ICE:

Do you decide to . . .

\ continue the discussion? *If yes, turn to page 42.*

\ bottle it up and try to distract Angel with kissage? *If yes, turn to page 43.*

You two sit on a gravestone marked SHIMERMAN, holding hands as you haltingly but honestly tell Angel that you are wigged about dying and afraid he'll go on to love someone else.

"That's not gonna happen," he tells you.

"We don't know that. I'm the Slayer. Slayers die."

"You won't," he insists. "You won't die."

"Angel." Your voice cracks. "Someday, I will. Even if I wasn't the Slayer, I'm a human being. We age. We . . . we have car accidents. We get sick. And I haven't been feeling all that hot lately. We're . . . mortal." You smile crookedly. "It's our curse."

"No, never say that," Angel says, touching your lips with his forefinger. "It's a blessing. Being human." He looks off into the distance. "I'd give a lot to be able to walk in the sunlight with you, Buffy. To get old with you."

"And gray?" you ask, smiling sadly at him. "And have all your teeth fall out?"

"Buffy, you're sixteen. You have your whole life ahead of you."

My whole life . . . could end tonight. "Come on, Angel, you know most slayers die before they're twenty."

"Not you."

SLAYER ACTION:
Turn to page 43.

You start kissing him so sweetly, and he responds . . . and you feel so close to him. It's so nice to know that if you died, he would be sad, and stay loyal to your memory.

Wait. Who are you kidding? *If* you die? Of course you're gonna die. Whether as a young slayer, or as a slightly older slayer who can legally drink bad beer, your future is . . . that you'll eventually be history.

And Angel will still be young and kissable. . . .

And suddenly it's all too much. The monsters and the things that don't stay dead, and Snyder and patrolling and training and everything. And it's like it's Angel's fault, or something. Because he isn't going to die!

"Who do you think you're leading on?" you fling at him as you wrench yourself out of his arms.

"What?" He reaches for you.

You cross your arms over your chest. "You . . . you don't . . . you're just . . . a guy! And that is . . . bad! Very bad!"

You pick a way bad fight. You tell yourself that 240-plus-year-old vampire or no, he really is just a guy, and guys are clueless; and he probably doesn't love you, anyway.

"You just pretend . . . you don't really . . . ," you go on, in babble mode.

"Are you saying I'm insincere?" he asks you.

"Call yourself whatever you want. Just don't call me!" Not that he does. He doesn't call. What is wrong with him that he doesn't call? Doesn't he have a phone? You don't know if he has a phone. How can you possibly be in love with a guy who doesn't have a phone?

"I'm out of here!" you shout. "And don't . . . write me any notes or flash signals against mountains, because I won't answer them!"

"What is wrong with you?" he demands, all forehead and dark hair and piercing dark eyes and frown.

"Nothing. Or maybe you! Yeah! You're wrong with me!"

You stomp off.

He lets you.

And that really sucks. Because of course he's not wrong with you. He's one of the few things that are right. . . .

You turn around to apologize. "Angel . . ."

But he's vanished into the night, the way he does.

Oh, Slayer. Here endeth a sucky lesson. Maybe you should have really done the patrol thing . . . or played the dutiful daughter and gone shopping with your mom. But you didn't. Dr. Laura would be all over you for doing the wrong thing. So you're alone in a cemetery with Mr. Pointy, and he's just not much on words.

Learn anything? Hope so.

Otherwise, it's just another Monday night in Sunnydale.

THE END

As you and your mom park the car and walk into the mall, you have your fingers crossed that Angel will wait for you in the cemetery. Your mom seems so happy to be out with you. You used to wonder why she and your dad didn't have any more kids.

Maybe once they saw how much trouble you were going to be, they decided to raise pets. Maybe that's why your mom always said yes when you would bring home a little kitten or a puppy. But here in Sunnydale, you and your mom don't have any pets. You're afraid they might die with all the weirdness. Willow has a fish tank.

She says fish are hard to kill. . . .

Still, it would be nice to have a brother or a sister. Probably a sister. A little sister.

Right. Who would do annoying things like try on your clothes with pizza fingers. . . .

You go up the same escalator that you first saw Lyle Gorch standing on with his dinner date. So to speak. You have a bit of a wiggins, but as your mom smiles at you, you smile back. She looks younger than she has in a long time. She's having fun!

The glittery doors of Shoe Planet beckon. The whole place glows like the Emerald City in *The Wizard of Oz.*

"Wow, what amazing decor!" your mom enthuses as you and she enter the store.

"Yeah," you agree. There are shoes lined from one side of the room to the other. Stilettos, flats, strappy sandals, hip boots. Shoe Planet's got 'em all.

It's got hotties for clerks, too. A totally *so* guy with dark hair and darker eyes walks up to you and Joyce and says, "Hi, I'm Danny. I'll be your personal footwear representative tonight. Are you looking for anything special?"

"Something sensible," your mom begins, and you wonder why she didn't just go to Nun Shoe Planet. Or Shoe Convent.

"Sure thing," Danny says. "And you?"

"Something sensible for my daughter as well," your mom says. You roll your eyes, and Danny grins at you.

"Something sensible in purple," you tell him. "And we have our flyer." Before you pull it out of your purse, you make sure there's nothing disgusting on it—it's been through a lot.

"That's fabulous," he chirps. He glances down at it. "CC. That would be another credit for Cordelia. She's up to free Bruno Maglis now!"

With a flourish, he takes the flyer and heads for the stockroom.

Wait a minute . . . something's wrong. Fishy, as Willow might say . . .

As Danny the personal shoe representative walks toward the stockroom, you realize that he is no shoe salesman! *He is only prentending to be one!*

SLAYER ACTI⊕N:
If you know how you know, turn to page 47.

If you don't know how you know,
turn to page 48.

That's right! Danny did not ask you and your mom for your shoe sizes! (Yours is a seven, by the way—same as Cordelia's.)

SLAYER ACTION:
Turn to page 49.

Turn to page 49.

Y ou don't know how you know that Danny is not what he seems, but you *know*. As you might say, your spider sense is tingling, although one thing you've wondered about is that first time you and Giles were in the Bronze together—well, not together together—and he said you'd develop some kind of sixth sense about this stuff, or at least about being able to tell when someone is a vampire. That's never really happened. The only reason you were able to save Willow from her skanky vampire ice-cream-luring dance partner was because his clothes belonged in the Smithsonian. Or maybe a John Travolta fan club charity event at the El Rey Theater in L.A.

Except maybe now you've got that sense, because you are so sure . . . !

Then your mom turns her head and says, "Oh look, honey. They're serving coffee drinks and pastries! What a lovely brass espresso machine!"

Yeah, against a wall of totally awesome boots with matching purses stands a lovely brass espresso machine that starts churning and foaming milk, and that Danny is now sauntering past . . . and is casting no reflection in!

No reflection?

Danny is not only an imposter . . . he's a vampire!

SLAYER ACTION:
Turn to page 49.

"**U**m, be right back, Mom," you say, and rush toward Danny. Halfway to the espresso machine, your mom looks at you quizzically.

"Is something wrong, Buffy?" she asks.

You put on the brakes. "Yes! Terribly wrong! I, ah, I forgot to tell Danny to also bring me some of the sensible shoes in red!" You turn to go.

"Well, that's not exactly a crisis," she replies. "He'll be back in a minute."

You brake again. "No, he won't!" As she frowns in puzzlement, you gesture at the excited throngs of fellow shoe customers. "He might not be able to find us again in this crowd!"

"Buffy, that wouldn't be such a tragedy. This place is lovely, yes, but it's just another shoe store."

You're getting desperate. "Mom, it's an entire *planet*. Of shoes."

"Girls and shoes . . . ," your mom murmurs, looking to the left.

You follow her gaze. Cordelia is with her Cordettes, and everyone is squealing over the four-inch buttercup-colored stilettos she's modeling. Wow. You can see why. They are the *kick*.

"Also, wanting something in sensible yellow," you say wistfully.

Then there's a scream.

"Stay here, Mom!" you cry.

Leaving your mom to conclude that you are a shoe addict (well, yes), you barrel in the direction of the scream.

You charge into the stockroom, to find Danny attacking another personal footwear representative! His hand is across her mouth, revealing two wide brown eyes. "Excuse me," he says, raising an eyebrow. His own eyebrow, to be more precise. "I'm reprimanding my subordinate. I caught her smoking!" he says.

His captive shakes her head in protest.

"It's like they say," you drawl, "you just can't hire good help these days."

He vamps. From her vantage point, his prey cannot see the vampire's face, but you sure can. "But you can suck the life out of them!" he rejoins.

Oh great—a comedian vampire shoe salesman imposter.

"You're the Slayer, right?" he asks brightly. "I was hoping you'd show! I was just gonna call it a night if you didn't. Leaving the walking bloodbags alone." He smiles wickedly. "But before I left, I was definitely going to snag some of those four-inch-high yellow stilettos that absolutely gorgeous brunette is buying. They just shout, 'Take me!' If they have them in my si . . . I mean, in size thirteen wide." He blushes a little. "For my . . . sister. Who has big feet."

"Right," you say slowly. "And she's also a . . ." You start to say "vampire," but realize that although his prisoner is freaking out, she cannot see his face. She is still conscious and listening to every word you say.

And you are supposed to stay a secret. *"A personal footwear representative."*

"Yes, she is. *A personal footwear representative,*" he replies, enjoying the game.

Great. By showing up at this grand opening, you may have saved the store from a case of employee theft—like he was going to pay for those size thirteens!—but you may have increased the chances of an employee death. And you had to race in here without a stake, didn't you? Of course you did.

Because you aren't supposed to even be here! You're supposed to be doing your Slayage duties!

Atop a neon pink shoe box, you spy one of those wood shoe tree things—the kind that keep shoes stretched and fresh. It looks to be about a size nine. You pick it up. With enough force, it could penetrate his chest.

"Let her go," you say to Danny.

He says, "Okay," and flings her right at you.

The girl is on a total collision course. But your Slayer reflexes kick in, just as Giles has honed them with training, and you grab hold of her before she can hurt herself.

She's panicking. You can see the glazed fear in her eyes. She doesn't know what to do. She probably doesn't even remember her own name.

You know that kind of fear. You remember it, from when your first Watcher—Merrick—taught you how to slay.

"Get out of here!" you shout at the girl.

She runs screaming out of the stockroom. You pick up the shoe tree and throw it as hard as you can at Danny.

He sees it coming and tries to duck.

Too late! It slams into his chest!

And he is dust!

"What the hell are you doing?" a voice behind you shouts.

You whirl around to discover an older man behind you with a name badge that reads D. GREENWALT, MANAGER.

"There was . . ." You turn back around, pointing . . . at nothing.

What can you say? You have nothing to say. Nothing to show. No way to defend yourself.

Then your mom pokes her head in the stockroom. Her eyes widen in horror at the big, terrible mess. "What's going on, Buffy?" she demands, her voice shrill. Before you can answer, she says to the manager, "Mr. Greenwalt, I'm Joyce Summers, and I am so sorry. Is there any damage? Of course we'll pay for it."

You hear that *we*. You dread that *we*. You have no idea what your mom's going to do to you, but you know it won't be shiny and fun.

Why can't I just tell her I'm the Slayer? you wonder miserably.

But you know why: It's part of the joy.

So you swallow hard and wonder if you should

bother making up some fake story, or simply leave with as much dignity as you can muster.

That wasn't supposed to be a stumper.

As you and your mom walk through the now-silent store, everyone is staring at you. One of Cordelia's Cordettes whispers in her ear, and Cordelia replies loudly, "How should I know what she was doing back there? It's like I told you before. She is a total psycho loony."

Your face feels like it's on fire. Gee, it would be nice if Cordelia stuck up for you. But then . . . she wouldn't be Cordelia.

Not that her being Cordelia is a good thing.

Her popular clique is watching you and murmuring. You hear someone whisper, "She burned down the gym at her school in L.A." And someone else mutters, "And she hangs out with that loser, Willow Rosenberg."

You cast a glance at your mother. She looks so angry and frustrated as you both leave the store. Tears are welling in her eyes.

"Mom," you begin.

"Please. Don't," Joyce says sadly.

In silence, you both walk out of the mall toward the car.

I should stick with the Slayage, you realize. *Every time I try to have a normal life . . . it's so not.*

"We can't move again," your mom says, half to herself. "I have the gallery, and, well, we just can't move again."

"I know, Mom. I'm sorry," you murmur. But she doesn't acknowledge you. It would be so much easier if you could just tell her your secret. But you can't.

So what can you do?

You can do better next time.

Chin up, Slayer. Tomorrow is another day.

If you survive the night.

THE END

Patrolling at SHS, just as Giles requested. There's a window in the science lab with a lock that you broke at the beginning of the year. You concealed the damage so well, the custodian hasn't noticed it, thus making it as convenient to sneak into school as it is to sneak out of your house. Not that sneaking into school is high on your list of funnest things ever.

But you're doing the right thing.

No distracting smoochies from Angel.

No new shoes with your mom.

And yet you're feeling dizzy and sick again. *Now, that's not fair.*

You wish you had a job where you could call in sick. It might be nice to get paid, too. You wonder what kind of shoes you might have ended up with if you had gone shopping with your mom.

Instead, you walk down the empty main corridor of the school, feeling most unwell, gazing at the stickers all over the lockers. Some are for bands. Some are for surfing companies. You look at the mural on the wall of the lounge.

Most of all, you listen. Marcie liked to play that sad song on the flute. You wonder if she ever went to band camp. Or if she had friends in her neighborhood, since she didn't have any in school.

Maybe wherever those scary guys in the suits took her, there were kids who liked her. You know what it's like to want some friends.

You used to be so popular back at Hemery.

You are so not, now.

Which is to the good. If you were popular, it would be a lot harder to have a secret identity. So hey, there's a plus.

And you do have friends. Wonderful friends. Willow and Xander are the best.

Click, click, click. Those are your heels on the Linoleum.

Tap, tap, tap . . .

You stop, cock your head. What is that?

Tap-tap-tap. Three quick taps.

"Hello?" you call.

Then *tap* . . . *tap.* More slowly.

Like a code. A code that you do not understand. A code they probably taught in a class you didn't attend.

Tap-tap-tap. Tap. Tap. Tap-tap-tap.

You are baffled. But you rise up on the balls of your feet and tiptoe so you can hear it better.

It's coming from the basement.

You head down toward the basement. As you descend the stairs you are feeling pretty wretched, really dizzy and sick, and you close your eyes and press your fingers against them.

Then you open them.

Oh.

My.

God.

Something has happened to the basement. Huge parts of it have collapsed—which must mean that parts of the school have collapsed! There is debris everywhere—splintered pieces of wood, a statue that you recognize from the trophy case upstairs . . . but all of it looks really old-fashioned.

And there is a big mound of that stinky stuff like before, with the Gorch brothers. You probably should go inspect it, but ewww . . .

SLAYER ACTION:
Turn to page 58.

You wish Willow were here with her little latex gloves and Velma-style forensics kit. You've seen her dissect all kinds of stuff in biology, and when she was about to cut into that baby Bezoar—ewww! Of course she was just pretending to do that so she could knock you senseless and drag you into a closet.

But she's not here, and you are.

And there's that thing about closets again. What is it with your friends and closets?

SLAYER ACTION:
Turn to page 72.

You walk to the stinky mound and crouch down beside it. It looks like leather, only very sparkly and rainbow-like. You pick up an old chair leg and poke at the leathery stuff with it.

It's like snakeskin.

Then you see something shiny sticking out of the ground. It looks as if it was buried, and that whatever shook the heck out of the basement popped it back up to the surface. It's kind of like a fancy salt shaker, only very large, maybe a foot long.

You walk toward it.

At that moment, Tector Gorch leaps from the shadows! He is fully vamped and ready for blood—yours.

Not to wig—you've still got your chair leg.

Let the good times roll!

"We meet again," he says, grinning.

"And again," you reply. You assume a slayer stance. But he just keeps racing toward you.

You're ready, but you could be readier. You're the first to admit that. But you're in the game, and that's what counts.

Then Lyle comes up right behind you! He's got his game face on too, and his cowboy hat.

Not a problem, you tell yourself. *The hat works for him.*

You begin to leap in the air, shooting out your leg for the roundhouse that will come after your three-sixty when, all of a sudden, there is a loud whoosh of air directly overhead and Lyle slams to the ground. "I gotta ghost on me, Tector!" he shouts.

Marcie Ross!

You race toward the downed vampire but his brother gets there first, grabbing hold of the invisible Marcie, who is also moaning. From his motions, you can see that she's not putting up much of a struggle.

Tector says, "Hey, this is a see-through human! I can smell her! But her blood smells funny!"

Then Tector sinks his teeth into her! But whoa, no fruit punch mouth! Her blood is invisible too.

"Yee-ha, Lyle!" Tector shouts. "This is some strange blood, hoss! Wait'll you have a slurp!"

"Sorry. Happy hour is over," you inform them as you reach Lyle and slam your fist into his face. He goes flying across the ruined basement and rams into a ruined piano, which clinks as he crashes into it.

Then you advance on Tector. He jumps up from the ground and backs away, hands extended. His gaze is on the piece of wood in your fist.

"Easy, now, Slayer," he says, as if he were talking to a bucking bronco. You are wicked crazy with anger. You don't get what's going on, and you need to see how badly Marcie is wounded. So to speak.

"What are you?" you demand of the vampire. "Why do you keep coming back? And why here?"

He looks nervously from you to his brother. "Lyle? You okay?"

"Ah shore am," Lyle says, disentangling himself from the piano. "You just keep her distracted and I'll be right there."

"He shouldn't be okay," you say through clenched teeth. "He should be dead."

Perhaps Lyle is sensing just how thoroughly pissed off you are. He takes off his hat and starts to back away. "Well, see, little gal—I mean, Miss Slayer—he is." He bobs his head. "We're vampires. Ah, Tector, let's get the hell out of here."

As he moves away you crouch down and touch Marcie. She is still invisible, and she is limp.

Lyle bolts . . . and you realize he's just trying to get away. You let him go. He is not your priority.

The invisible girl is.

Except . . . Marcie is becoming visible!

Yes, there she is, lying on the ground! You drop to your knees and gaze at her as she comes into focus. Her short, brownish hair . . . her regular features . . . you realize even now that you still might have trouble picking her out of a crowd.

Her throat has been torn open by fangs, and those fangs did a real job on her. Blood from her wound is pooling beneath her. There is a lot of it.

You put your hand over the injury to her neck. It's coming out too fast. There's an awful lot of it. Too much.

These are things a slayer knows.

Her eyes flutter open. They are wide and unfocused.

"It's okay," you say. "It's going to be all right."

But you are lying.

You know you're lying as you check her pulse.

Marcie Ross is dying.

You start to pick her up. Getting her out of here is

your priority. Then Lyle says, "Wait a minute, what are we doing, brother? Are we Texans or not?"

"We shore are!" Tector informs him.

"Then let's get her!"

You glance over your shoulder. The Gorches are headed straight for you!

You can probably outrun them, even with Marcie in your arms. It would probably be the best thing to do.

But then Lyle says to Tector, "Shoot, we're gonna kill us a slayer, Tector! Then Sunnydale will be one big slaughterhouse!"

"Even if'n we don't, we can still move on in here! We can open up fer biznis! Sell grain-fed blood all over the country!" Tector replies.

You so don't like what you are hearing.

So what do you do? Keep running, or stop and fight the Gorch brothers? What's your priority? Saving a life now, or potentially saving a lot of lives later?

And what about solving the mystery of how these guys keep coming back?

SLAYER CHOICE:

Do you decide to . . .

❚ keep running with Marcie? *If yes, turn to page 76.*

❚ stop and fight the Gorches? *If yes, turn to page 77.*

It's pitch black. You have no idea where you're going. You heft the piece of wood in your hand. It's suddenly more than something to dust vampires with. It's your only weapon against the unknown.

You're moving along; your foot knocks into something on the ground. Something that gives way.

Something kind of squishy.

You have no idea what it is, but it's not moving and it's not screaming. You squat and poke at it experimentally.

The piece of wood pierces it, and a horrible, noxious odor permeates the space around you.

You know that you have just encountered something dead . . . something that's not likely to give you any problems.

You start to rise . . . and this time, you step on something hard. You run the ball of your boot along it.

It feels like a tree branch . . . or a bone.

The hair on the back of your neck sticks straight up. You so do not want to bend down again and do some further exploration, but you have to. This may be evidence that the monster that is eating people and spitting out their bones has come this way.

SLAYER ACTION:

If you're looking for Ampata, turn to page 58.

*If you're looking for Marcie Ross,
turn to page 235.*

But another wave of dizziness overcomes you. A blue light shimmers around you.

You see the basement again, shimmering in blue. No broken pieces of furniture, no ruined piano. But it's still very different. There are some wooden crates against the far wall. They're labeled SHS YEARBOOKS, 1937.

"Marcie?" you call. Your voice sounds distant, almost as if you're underwater.

But there are two shapes in the distance. One is tall; the other is the strange, hunched figure you saw earlier, peering into the basement. Apparitions? More dead things, come back to menace the living?

"Who . . . who . . . ?" It's becoming difficult to talk. You are very ill. Sweat breaks out across your forehead.

You bend over and retch.

You stagger on.

Then you hear a strange murmuring coming from the shapes. It rises in pitch; it is frantic. It sounds like people trying to shout past hands clasped across their mouths.

Blue light wells and sparkles around them; it quivers and expands like jellyfish.

You stumble forward. You're losing consciousness. So not a good idea right now.

"Marcie," you whisper, "I'm so sorry."

Then you drop to your knees.

And then you drop to the ground.

SLAYER ACTION:
Turn to page 65.

"**B**uffy?" calls a voice.

You open your eyes to find Willow kneeling beside you.

"Will," you say groggily. You slowly sit up.

"Oh God, Buffy! We thought we'd lost you," she says. Her eyes are brimming with joy. She takes your hand. "C'mon."

You're in the basement. It's the basement you know and loathe: the basement of Sunnydale High School. "Marcie," you say.

You run to where you think you left her.

There is nothing there. Not even blood.

"What?" You're terribly distressed. "Where is she?"

"C'mon, Buffy," Willow urges. "Let's get out of here."

"But, Marcie . . . ," you protest.

"Is not here. I combed this place searching for you." She tugs at your hand.

"But . . ." You keep glancing around.

"Buffy," Willow goes on, "your mom called my house, looking for you. I told her we were studying really late last night and you fell asleep." She makes a little face. "I'm not very good at lying. You know it makes me nervous."

"Thanks, Will," you say.

"Also? She wants you to call her at the gallery." Willow bites her lower lip the way she does when she's anxious. "She sounded pretty pissed."

"I wish I could just tell her I'm the Slayer," you

say. "It would make my complicated life, not."

"It would still have complications," Willow argues. "Just different ones." She smiles faintly. "Like, 'I have to patrol now, Mom.' 'Did you eat? Want me to pack you a snack?'"

You're freaking out inside, but you try to hold it together. Marcie was dying. Where is she now?

But the Scooby way is to banter. So you do.

"That would actually be kind of nice. There are no slayer hangout places for when I'm on patrol. Cops hog the doughnut shops."

"What about the Espresso Pump?" Willow suggests.

"Nah, too obvious. I can just hear someone asking my mom, 'What was your daughter doing here last night at midnight?'"

"Yeah, I guess you're right," she says. Then she brightens. "*I* could pack you a snack. Do you like animal crackers? I love 'em. And one of those little cartons of milk."

But you can't keep up the banter. You are seriously conflicted. As you and Willow walk together, you're so grateful she's your friend. You can't imagine what your life would be like without her. She's someone you can depend on. Someone to do all the girlie stuff with: talk about boys, paint your toenails, sit in your jammies with Mr. Gordo on your lap and try to understand while she tutors you in the math. . . .

"Will, you'll always be you—right? I mean, you won't turn out to be a vampire or a demon or something, will you?" You look anxiously at her.

She raises her brows. "Buffy, this is me, remember? I'm just the faithful, boring sidekick."

"Not boring," you insist.

"No, no. Boring is good," she tells you. "I mean, I used to dream of having an exciting life. Like factoring polynomials, only more intense." Her mischievous grin clues you in that she's pushing the nerd Q a little high for your benefit.

"Then I met you, Buffy, and no offense, but there are days when I miss boredom. Even though Xander was always better at it than me. Because if I don't have anything to do, I just reread my textbooks. Or rather, I used to, before I started hacking into the coroner's office and stuff like that. I must be the only person in Sunnydale who has disaster sites bookmarked as favorites."

She shakes her red hair. "I'm not complaining, mind you. I'm really glad you're my friend, Buffy."

"That's so nice to know," you tell her. Your voice cracks. "Because, oh Willow, I feel so terrible. I should have been able to save her."

You break down.

And Willow holds you.

SLAYER ACTION:
Turn to page 68.

In the library. Giles and the gang—Xander, Willow, and Cordelia, even—try to cheer you up as you tell them what happened. "I can't believe I failed," you tell them.

"It could have happened to any of us," Giles comforts you.

"No, it couldn't. Because we are not vampire slayers," Cordelia cuts in. "We are normal high school students . . . well, no, none of you is a normal high school student. I am the only normal person in this room! Oh God, what am I doing here?" She begins to panic.

"What are you going to do?" Willow asks you. At her urging, you called your mom. Things are . . . okay. Not great, but not "you-are-grounded," either. But that's not highest on your list of problems right now.

SLAYER ACTION:

If you fought the Gorches, turn to page 79.

If you ran with Marcie in your arms,
turn to page 69.

Giles says, "I'll call the Watchers Council for advice."

"Why bother?" Xander says angrily. "All they do is put you on hold."

As Willow whispers, "It's all right," Giles walks over to the phone and dials a number. He says, "Yes, I'd like . . . yes, I'll hold."

"It's going to be all right," Willow says.

If only you had trained harder and paid better attention to Giles's boring lectures on . . . whatever he lectures you about, this would never have happened. You could have lasted longer, even though you felt sick. Or you would have known what the shimmering was all about, or who the shapes were. A lazy, distracted slayer is a slayer in big, big trouble.

"Yes, I'll hold," Giles says wearily into the phone.

"I don't want to slay anymore," you grump sadly.

"Maybe you could emigrate to Canada," Xander says to you. "I have an uncle who moved there. They need skilled craftspeople, and hey, you whittle." He gestures to a stake lying on the table. You sharpened it yourself.

"Your uncle went to Canada to avoid the draft," Willow points out.

"Buffy got drafted," Xander says. "I'm sure the Watchers Council is a vicious right-wing conspiracy." He winks at you. "You could conscientiously object."

"Well, actually, I've been holding for quite some time." Giles's voice is rising. In Britishese, that means he's irritated and tempted to speak rudely. But will not.

Because he's British.

"Buffy did not get drafted by the right wing of anything," Cordelia drawls. "She was chosen. Selected. Picked out. Like a fairy princess. Only, no fairy godmother to show you how to dress."

"Hey," you protest.

Giles whips off his glasses and says, to whomever is on the other end of the phone, "I have waited bloody long enough!"

"Wow! I've never seen him so dynamic," Xander drawls.

"*Thank* you," Giles says, exasperated. "Yes, Rupert Giles. Yes, I'm the librarian. Yes. I'm inquiring about Marcie Ross. Yes, the student. Yes. I want to make sure she is still accounted for. I see. Thank you very much."

He slowly puts down the phone and turns around to face you. "I didn't keep you informed about this—I thought it would be better to dismiss all thought of Marcie from your minds, such as they are—but Marcie was taken to a sort of training camp after her capture. For, ah, assassins. For your government. And they say that Marcie is in class at this very moment."

You are so surprised—and relieved, and confused—that your head tingles. Alive? So you didn't fail her after all?

"Class? In assassin training? How can that be?" Willow asks.

"The Watchers Council is spying on her?" Xander adds.

Giles looks a little uncomfortable, like he's revealing classified information. He pushes up his glasses and says, "We have an operative keeping tabs on her, yes."

"Wow. Watchers can be spies," Willow says, looking excited. She frowns anxiously at Giles. "Are *you* a spy? Never mind. Too nosy." She flashes you a look that says, *Is he a spy?*

"I assure you, I am no spy," Giles replies. "I am far too busy serving as Buffy's Watcher to do anything else. But, more important, Marcie Ross is alive and well. She didn't die in the basement, no matter what you saw or experienced, Buffy."

SLAYER ACTION:
Turn to page 73.

Thought du jour:

Cordelia and friendship: quicksand, or the beach at low tide?

SLAYER ACTION:

If you're in the basement with the stinky mound, turn to page 59.

If you're looking for Ampata, turn to page 107.

Everyone's eyebrows raise. A sense of relief fills the room. Your knees practically buckle, and you sit heavily on the nearest chair.

It makes a kind of sense, you think. *Look how the Gorches kept coming back. They're some kind of doubles or something.*

"How can they be sure she's there? Maybe someone's filling in for her, pretending to be her," Cordelia says.

She has a point. You feel anxious all over again. "They can't even see her! For all they know, no one is sitting in her chair," you add. "The lump in her bed? Invisible pillow!"

"They tell me they have incontrovertible evidence that she is accounted for," Giles announces.

You blink. "They gave her a convertible?"

"That's not fair! Buffy hasn't even rated a driver's license! Our superhero is better than their supervillain any day!" Xander says.

"I suppose one may argue that Marcie Ross is a villain no longer, since her . . . activities are rather on the scale of those of a special agent. One could venture that in a sense, they are rehabilitating her," Giles asserts, looking put upon. "Trying to help her fit into society."

"Well, thank you, Chairman Mao," Xander shoots back. "Here in the land of the free, we don't believe in rehabilitation. We think it's our God-given right to stay as screwed up as we want to be."

"Which would explain your lack of social acceptance," Cordelia offers, smiling at Xander. "And maybe your clothes, too."

"Hey, at least I don't have a platinum card at Hookers "R" Us!"

"Closet?" Cordelia murmurs, with a note of triumph in her voice.

Giles whips off his glasses again, cleans them, and peers at the lenses as he holds them up to the light. "At the risk of interrupting this fascinating conversation, or perhaps in the hope of it, I suggest we reconvene after classes to do some research."

The hills are not alive.

"Me too?" you ask.

Cordelia raises her hand. "I have cheerleading practice."

Willow makes a face. "And my parents are taking me to a sort of Jewish social group with a common interest." This does not appear to be happiness-making.

"How lovely," Giles says, smiling at your best friend. "What is your group's common interest?"

"Keeping our homes safe," she explains. "Because of, well, Sunnydale and all."

"Oh, like a Jewish Neighborhood Watch?" Cordelia asks. She smiles. "Since we live in a gated community, we don't have to worry about stuff like that." Then she frowns. "Except for all the gardeners and housekeepers and nannies and people like that. You have to watch them like a hawk."

"Cordelia Chase, champion of the people," Xander says snidely.

"Well, it's true! They are poor, Xander." Her eyes

practically spit fire at him. "Naturally they want our stuff! Don't you?"

"Your stuff? No way." His eyes are spitting fire back. It's a very good thing there are no marshmallows in the library. Because they would be *toast*.

Actually, they would still be marshmallows—just toasted marshmallows . . . or marshmallows that are burnt to a cinder. . . .

"All right. That's enough." Giles sounds all headachy. "Since some of you are otherwise occupied tonight, let's reconvene tomorrow. I shall do some research."

Yes! you think. *A night off!*

"And you should come in for a training session, Buffy," he adds. He cocks his head. "Unless you have a familial obligation tonight as well."

"A . . . what?"

"If your mom wants you to stay home or go somewhere with her," Willow translates helpfully.

Why couldn't Giles just say that?

"Well, do you?" Giles presses. "You know, you don't look at all well. Do you want to go to the nurse's office?"

SLAYER CHOICE:

Do you decide to . . .

❭ train? *If yes, turn to page 85.*

❭ go see the nurse? *If yes, turn to page 22.*

"**K**eep living," you murmur to Marcie as you tighten your grip on her limp form and put on the turbo. But she's bleeding so badly. You just don't know if you have enough time.

"Come back here, Slayer!" Lyle yells at you. "You chicken, or whut?"

You don't waste your breath. You keep running.

Then suddenly a wave of extreme nausea hits and you're forced to stop and put Marcie down . . .

. . . *oh no* . . .

SLAYER ACTION:
Turn to page 78.

Carefully, you set down Marcie. Then you whirl around. It's Slayer time!

You take on Lyle first. He wants to fight. He's grinning, and you want to take that cowboy hat off his head and shove it . . . er, wipe that smile right off his face.

Suddenly, you are so angry. Isn't it enough that you fought these guys one time? Do you have to keep doing it again and again?

Your rage communicates itself to Lyle, whose smile fades.

"Okay, then," he murmurs, "show me what you got."

"What I got," you respond, "is this!"

You hold the chair leg over your head, do a total banzai run at him, charging like a wild bull or a crazed stallion or maybe even a pissed-off, um, you don't know that much about cowboy-type analogies, but you are so angry, so very, very furious, so much fury, they should probably call you Ms. Fury, except you are Ms. Slayer—and slam your fist into Lyle's face!

. . . And stake him!

"Stay dead," you warn him as he dusts. "Or you'll be sorry!"

Then you take off after Tector, who's already headed up the stairs. You are going to beat him to a pulp, and then you are going to end him!

But he's had a head start.

SLAYER ACTION:
Turn to page 78.

You are feeling sick again; you're reeling, and you stumble over a pile of dirt. Your head snaps back as you try to keep your footing, and you see a huge hole in the ceiling. Three figures are staring down at you: two tall, and one short and hunched over. You can't make out anything more.

Then someone—or something—moves behind you.

You suddenly feel cold and anxious. Your body shivers hard; you can feel yourself going black.

No. No, I can't, you think. *I have to save Marcie.*

Then you go blind. You can't see anything.

SLAYER ACTION:
Turn to page 63.

Her panic processed, Cordelia eagerly raises her hand into the air. "So, Marcie has disappeared—well, you know what I mean—and you think it's your fault because you stopped to fight the Gorches. If you go to jail, can I have those black sandals you wore to the Bronze last Friday?" At the perplexed looks of the others, she says, "Please. They're the only decent pair of shoes she owns." She smiles at you. "You wouldn't want them to rot in your closet while you're rotting in jail, right?"

"Jail." Xander shakes his head. "I've seen the movies. There will be bulky matrons with short haircuts who'll give you extra cigarettes for . . . favors."

"I don't smoke, Xander," you remind him.

He looks at you sadly. "You will," he murmurs. "You will."

Gulp.

"We'll try to figure this out," Giles assures you. "I'll call the Council, see what is to be done. . . ."

"They'll make her go to jail," Cordelia says decisively. "Now, about the shoes. . . ."

"You have a one-track mind," Xander hisses at her. She smiles lazily at him. "And you don't?"

Xander is undaunted. "You already have so many shoes, you probably have to rent storage containers for them."

"No. They're lined up on special shelves that go from the top to the bottom of my closet," Cordelia replies. She gazes straight at him. "My bedroom closet."

"Your closet," Xander murmurs, like he's being hypnotized.

Cordelia's eyes half close. "Yes, my closet."

"What is wrong with you people?" Willow demands, rising from her chair. "Buffy's going to jail and all you can talk about is shoes and closets?"

"She is not going to jail!" Giles insists.

SLAYER ACTION:
Turn to page 69.

The temptation of Cordelia and her flyers is of the past.

It's school, it's Monday, and Xander and Willow catch up to you.

"Hi, Buffy!" Willow says cheerily. She's in a plaid jumper, tights, and track shoes. You remember Cordelia's cutting remark about Willow and the softer side of Sears the first day you met them both. Will's just Will, and you have grown to love her sense of style. Actually, you have grown to love *her*. She's your best friend. You really don't care what she wears, which is so not the pre-Slayage Buffy of the L.A. days.

You have definitely grown as a person!

"You are so much the Buffalator I was hoping to see," Xander adds, as the two fall into step with you. Tall, with curly dark hair, his skateboard under his arm, he's got on an oversize plaid shirt and baggy pants, also typical for him.

"Hi, guys," you say brightly. If anything can cheer you up on the first day of a looooong school week, it's your two buds. "Will, you are so giddy and up."

Willow nods, blue eyes shiny. "I'm so excited! Today we're discussing the limit!"

You blink. "The limit? On what?"

"On personal freedom," Xander grouses. "Since we are sentenced to six hours of torment in this gulag. And that's just today."

"The limit is a mathematical concept," Willow says patiently. "Having nothing to do with torment—"

"That's a matter of opinion, about which I have

nothing to say," Xander cuts in. He turns to you. "For you, I have news. Giles wants to see you right away."

"Now?" you squeak. Seeing you "right away" usually bodes of the bad. Giles asking to see you first thing in the morning is like Principal Snyder asking to see you anytime.

"I'll cover for you in health class," Willow tells you. "I'll tell Ms. Kalosh you're ill."

"Not healthy for health. That always works," Xander adds helpfully.

"Serious. There's something going around," Willow continues earnestly. "Everyone is getting it. People are barfing all over the place. Or, actually, in the bathrooms. I was here yesterday with Miss Calendar, working in the computer lab, and three people had to go home to throw up."

"Gee, yet more to look forward to as we begin the week," Xander drawls. "Next, we'll all be breaking out in boils."

"We can hope. Not," you say. "Maybe Giles just wants to tell me he's going home too." At that thought, you break out in hope.

"Yeah, maybe he's puking his guts out," Xander says archly. "We can hope."

"Oh, you know I don't wish any badness on him. Just . . . I need a break," you tell your friends with a sigh.

"He does push you awfully hard," Willow says loyally.

"Buffy's the Slayer. She's supposed to *do* the pushing," Xander concludes.

The warning bell rings. Willow and Xander move off with the rest of the herd, and you give a little wave as you head for the library. In an attempt to appear all happy Slayer, you breeze through the double doors and say, "Hi, Giles. What's up?"

There he is, Rupert Giles, Watcher Extraordinaire and spokesmodel for tweed, reading a big, heavy, dusty book bound in leather.

How new. How different.

He looks up at you and says, "Ah. Buffy. Good."

"I am," you agree. "I am Buffy, and I am good."

"Well, that remains to be seen, doesn't it?" he says a bit frostily. "I've been noticing a deterioration in your slaying lately. I think we need to double up on your training sessions."

Just Say No.

Just say it.

Say it, Buffy. You have free will!

"Oh," you answer, with a minor thrust of the lower lip. Which used to work on your dad. When you were five. It never worked on your mom.

It doesn't appear to work on Giles. It doesn't even register with Giles.

"Good. I'm glad we had this little chat," he says, resuming his reading. At least he's not all sarcastic, the way Snyder gets whenever he says nearly the exact same words. As he wanders back to his office, he says over his shoulder, "I'll see you tonight, yes?"

"Um. Okay. I have to go home to help my mom unpack some African tribal masks. Then I'll do that which I should do." You hesitate. "Or maybe I could patrol. We still haven't found that monster that's chomping everyone and leaving just skin and bones."

"That's also a plan," he concurs. "Either of those things will be most useful as we battle the forces of darkness."

Think about that, Slayer. The more you train, the better Slayer you will be.

But patrol . . . has its appeal as well.

SLAYER CH⊕ICE:

Do you decide to . . .

\ come back to train? *If yes, turn to page 85.*

\ go on patrol? *If yes, turn to page 86.*

Quarterstaffs?

"Hello, Giles? I'm not going to be fighting Friar Tuck," you say.

Attired in a helmet and knee and shoulder pads, he makes a speech about traditions being handed down through the ages blah-blah-blippidy-blah that would have Kendra welling up with tears of pride, and then you two start smacking each other.

Only . . . not for long. Then it's Buffy smacking Giles.

He says, "Okay, yes. I guess we're done, then."

"Patrol?" you ask him.

He looks impressed. "I'm pleased to see you taking your duties so seriously," he says. "You're becoming an excellent slayer."

Praise from Giles! It's so . . . new!

"Thank you!" you chirrup.

And you sail out the door. You are a very good Buffy!

SLAYER ACTION:
Turn to page 86.

Oh, Slayer. Bad girl.

You are supposed to be on patrol. And this is not really patrolling, now, is it?

After you helped your mom with the tribal masks for her gallery, you put on the black trousers and the black turtleneck sweater and the knitted cap. Checked the mirror: You have a sort of Caroline-Corrs-when-she's-blond vibe going on, which is good—you'll drum those stakes right into the vamps tonight!

But then Angel offered to come on patrol with you. He showed just as you were crawling out your bedroom window and dropping daintily into the bushes like a paratrooper in a movie where all the characters are men and they wear khaki and not boots with pointy heels. There he was, all with the dark hair and eyes, and, to paraphrase Cordelia, even though, ew, Cordelia: "Hello, salty goodness!"

Angel said calmly, "Going out?"

"Just patrolling," you managed to reply. You know he can hear your heartbeat; you hoped he thought it was thundering so hard because of the jump from the roof . . . and not because he looked so amazing in the moonlight. Dark sweater, dark trousers, black leather jacket.

"Want some company?"

"Sure. Who?" you quipped. "But I'm on the job," you reminded him.

So . . . you said yes. However, you made it clear that you were on patrol. You were doing your Slayer thingie. You were being good Buffy.

And for a while, you guys patrolled as a team just great. Really. Just like the night he slept on the floor in your room, Angel was a perfect gentleman. When you got to cemetery number three, he yanked off the padlock on the wrought-iron gate that read HAPPY MEMORIES MEMORIAL GARDENS in fancy scrolled letters and pushed it open with a flourish.

The curlicue metal went *squeeeeeakkkkk,* and he winced at the noise—vampires have good hearing, hence the hearing of heartbeats—then you smiled up at him and wondered if he could tell that you had just spent your entire allowance on some new Smash Box makeup, including a shade of foundation that Willow said was *perfecta* but now you were worried maybe looked wrong in moonlight.

But now, here you are, just inside the gate, and he is looking at you like you look good enough . . . um, not to chomp on, but to maybe . . . kiss. He has such soulful eyes—okay, you lied when you told him that in your diary you meant to call them bulging. Plus, he is *almost smiling.* This rare event is worthy of a diary entry all its own.

You join him on the cemetery grounds, and he swings the door shut.

Squeeeeeeakkkkk.

Okay. Deep breath, Buffy. Let's focus. You try to pull yourself back into Slayage mode. The devouring of people is a bad thing. Your job is to stop things of the bad. And you'll stop them tonight!

In unison, you begin to walk, your boots crushing

desiccated leaves. There are lots of leaves. The trees shiver as if they're cold and afraid, but it's the wind, just the wind.

Happy Memories is not your usual cemetery. Instead, there's lots of variety, and some really memorable tourist attractions. Oh, you've got your typical angels weeping on headstones and your standard "Rest in Peace, My Beloved" types of sayings on the marble. But then you notice the funny grave topped with a foot-high statue of a man aiming a ball at a set of finger-tall bowling pins. Etched in stone, it reads TODD MCINTOSH, BOWLING WITH GOD, and the dates of his birth and death.

You have heard that there's also a woman buried in the pink Cadillac she won for selling the most door-to-door beauty products in Sunnydale, but Giles insists that it's just an urban legend.

"And a terribly sad statement on the effect of consumerism on the American psyche," he was quick to add.

What*ever.*

"Hope we don't strike out tonight," Angel says as you walk past Todd McIntosh's bowling-themed grave. He glances up at the moon, whose radiant glow highlights his chiseled bone structure. He's got the best nose. "You need to go home soon."

"I have an hour or two to spare," you answer. You point to another choice grave—the mausoleum of Violet "Candy" Jones, which is covered with stone flowers. Arched over the entrance to the mausoleum read the words MY DARLING VIOLET. Xander has made jokes about "my shrinking violet" and my "stinking violet," but tonight, you're glad Violet was someone's darling. Everyone should be someone's darling.

"So . . . not much going on, looks like," you say. "No sign of a monster thing that's chomping people and leaving just their skin and bones."

Angel turns to look at you as if he's about to say something, but remains silent. You tell yourself that you're looking for monsters, but face it, Buffy— what you're looking for is a little romance. The moon overhead casts Angel's oh-so-perfect features in ivory and shadow. If he'd just kiss you, and tell you that he loves you, you could forget for a little while that you're the Slayer. You could just be a normal sixteen-year-old girl . . . his girl.

You'd carry a happy memory like that to your grave. Hopefully, not an early grave, but hey, Slayer, there will be a grave involved someday. . . .

But not tonight. It's far too nice a night to die.

Then he puts his lips against yours—they're a little cool, but soft—and thoughts about the mission kind of drift away.

You kiss back. And back again. And with more backage . . .

You are so forgetting why you're there.

"Angel," you whisper eagerly, clinging to him as he enfolds you in his arms.

Whoa . . . you are losing it.

But not necessarily in a good way.

You feel kind of dizzy—a little sick, even. Everything is going fuzzy as you kiss Angel like you've never kissed him before. It's feels as if the world is swirling around you while you spin in a tiny circle— even though you are standing still.

Much with the swirling.

If this is love, okay, but who knew there should be Alka-Seltzer involved? You kind of sink against Angel as your knees buckle. Your intense desire for him gives way to, um, an intense desire to barf.

Angel is clearly unaware of the nausea. He's way smooching you and you think you're going to have to tell him to stop, except that he pulls away and says passionately, "We should be killing something."

Which is a good, helpful reminder, because—

—the Master and his head vampire minion, Luke, are racing around the corner of Darling Violet's mausoleum and heading straight toward you!

But I dusted them both!

"Slayer!" the Master exults, and he hurtles himself right at you. You can smell him in all his evil, pasty, bat-face glory, separated at birth from Principal Snyder, except for the black leather fashion statement.

The Master so terrified you that you dreamed of him all summer. Then you came home to discover his followers attempting to resurrect him. You staked Absalom, the ringleader, and then you took a big old mallet over to the bones of the Master and you wailed on them like there was no tomorrow—for him! You sobbed and you slammed down that thing until his bones were ground into dusty bits of dustiness!

But the Master's back!

And so is Luke! That makes no sense. You dusted Luke at the Bronze. You saw him explode. So . . . he *cannot* be here!

However, he's not exploding now as he thrashes through the piles of dead leaves and laughs like this is all some great big party and you are a Slayer-shaped piñata. He runs into Todd McIntosh's gravestone, and the bowling pins break off and go flying in all directions.

"Buffy, go!" Angel shouts, and you move away from him to give yourself more room to fight.

"I'm all set!" you shout back. Legs spread for balance, arms outstretched—*aiya!*—your Slayer blood rises. You were born for this, for the fighty-fighty-fight-fight.

Then Angel yells, "No! I mean, you get the hell out of here! *Go!* This shouldn't be happening!"

"Hello? Denial is evil!" you shout back, keeping your eyes on the prize.

Angel persists. "You know what I mean! You should go!"

Señorita Slayer, your machisma is offended. Angel knows you're not some damsel in distress in a cheesy polyester nightgown who needs defending. You are the Slayer!

You think about saying, "Hey dude, I'll retreat if *you* do!"

You also think about saying, "Fine! I'm outta here! Witness my leaving!"

Or you could remind him that you are the Slayer in a nicer way than calling him "dude," and also, that approaching the two of you are things of evil that need your special touch of flying fatality.

But this is not usually Angel's style—he's no vampire chauvinist—so maybe things are far scarier than meets the eye!

So . . . it seems you have a choice to make.

SLAYER CHOICE:

Do you decide to . . .

\ go surfer speak on Angel? *If yes, turn to page 93.*

\ flounce away? *If yes, turn to page 101.*

\ just deal with it and fight? *If yes, turn to page 95.*

"**H**ey dude, I'll retreat if *you* do!" you snap at your true beloved.

"How old are you, twelve?" Angel shoots back, looking amazed. "And you're saying 'dude' now? Are you, what, a surfer?"

You are . . . miffed! He's stealing your lines!

And of course at that moment, the Master turns to Luke and says, "Let's just stand here a moment, shall we, and give them some screen time alone. Because their clever banter just screams for some close-ups. Particularly when the Slayer's new makeup is so fresh and dewy."

SLAYER ACTION:
Turn to page 94.

Excuse me? How old *are* you?

Do you think this is some game? Some TV show? Some TV game show? Do you actually think you have time to pick a fight with Angel over anything right now? That Luke and the Master will take a commercial break while you spank Angel's inner puppet, er, moppet—oh, that still sounds so wrong—and get him straight on the factoids about today's grrlpowerful world?

I think not, Buffy.

Because here's what happens when you do take a station break from sanity and start going all diva:

You stomp your boot like some moronic cheerleader—okay, you were a cheerleader back at Hemery, and you wanted to be a cheerleader here, and hey, much stomping, all of it synchronized and therefore challenging and requiring much practice, so not moronic—

Anyway, you stomp your foot. Twice. On a grave slab so old, the name and dates have worn clean off.

And guess what happens?

SLAYER ACTION:
Turn to page 102.

As you whip out a stake and get ready to fight, the Master sneers at you and says, "The Slayer, eh? You're dressed rather oddly. But I like your makeup."

"There's a plus," you retort. "Wanna go to the prom? I did, after I killed you the first time!"

"What are you talking about?" He seems genuinely—if only momentarily—confused. "We've never met before. In fact . . ." He looks around. He sees the date on Darling Violet's mausoleum and gestures toward it with one of his cracked, peeling, yucky fingernails. "Can it be nineteen ninety-nine?" he says, sounding stunned.

"Of course not, Master!" Luke shouts. "It's nineteen thirty-seven! The year that we will open the Hellmouth!"

"Yes! Yes!" The Master grins at Angel. "Come to help?" Angel glances at you. You give him a nod.

And . . . action!

You and Angel move into synchronized battle mode. There are two of you, and two bad guys—great odds for you, bad odds for the baddies. Which is as it should be.

The Big Noise is out for blood—yours—as he attacks with full fury. His breath is almost as icky as his white, batlike face, and you remember what it felt like when he bit you. It hurt, and there was nothing you could do about it. The memory of that has haunted you. And now here he is, and you are more than ready for payback. You destroyed his bones, but he has continued to haunt you. Now you have another shot at exorcising him from your life for good.

You drop into a crouch and sweep a powerful half-circle with your right leg. Success! You catch him behind the heels and throw him off his feet. He falls on his back; you whip a stake out of your pea coat as you leap on top of him. You arc it over your head and slam it down as hard as you can into his chest.

He explodes into dust!

"Ha!" you shout. It is a sweet moment, and you savor it. But only for a second; you leap up just in time to see Angel chop-sock Luke right in the smacker. Back Luke staggers, back-back-back, and *wham!* Angel pushes Luke up against the side of a tomb with a satisfying sound of breaking bones. You really hope it hurt.

"Angel!" you yell, and throw him a stake. He catches it easily and stabs his adversary directly in the heart.

Luke and the Master are history . . . again, and as you catch your breath, Angel hurries to your side and says, "Buffy, are you all right?"

You slide into his embrace and look up at him. "I'm fine. But how did those guys come back? Is there such a thing as a re-resurrection spell?"

Angel shakes his head. His dark eyes are troubled. "Not that I know of. You need to talk to Giles right away."

"I will." You're pumped from the fight; adrenaline is coursing through your veins. You're aware of every place his body touches yours, and you swallow hard and say, "I will . . . right . . . away . . . in a little while."

Angel hesitates. "You should probably get home. You can call him from your room."

You slide your arms around his neck. "But we destroyed them, Angel. They're gone. So . . . we deserve to celebrate. Don't you agree?"

You know he's weakening. He wants to celebrate as much as you do. He bends his head down to kiss you; you lift your head . . . and he says, "Are you sure, Buffy? It's your decision."

SLAYER CH⊕ICE:

Do you decide to . . .

hold off the celebration and go home? *If yes, turn to page 98.*

postpone going home so you can stay with Angel in the cemetery? *If yes, turn to page 99.*

"**Y**ou're right," you say wearily. "I should go home."

Angel walks with you, which is pretty nice. You climb up the tree toward your room. Then you wave good night as you cross over the sill.

You start to pick up the phone, but then you hear your mom's footsteps in the hall. As quickly as you can, you put down the phone, pull on your pajamas, and climb into bed.

She raps on your door.

"Come in," you say quickly.

"Hi." She looks very relieved to see you. "I phoned. I guess you didn't hear it. For a minute I thought maybe you weren't . . . here."

That I had snuck out.

"No," you say, all innocence. "Sometimes I sleep very soundly."

She takes that in. "I didn't know that. I've actually been wondering if we should go to the doctor for your insomnia. Oh, there's so much I don't know about you, Buffy." She sighs, then brightens. "But I'm glad to hear you have some good nights."

SLAYER ACTION:
Turn to page 131.

"Let's take a moment to smell the flowers . . . on the graves," you say, settling down for some good kisses. What could be better than that?

Fog wafts around your feet and rises to both your waists. It's getting chilly, and as you kiss Angel, you shiver slightly.

"Maybe you should get home," Angel says into your ear. "You could catch your death."

And suddenly you are thinking about death. During kissing.

Wait a minute. I'm having a very bad déjà vu experience.

"Angel," you say, "no death discussions, all right?"

"What's wrong?" he asks, pulling away. "Is there something you aren't telling me? Something else that's happened?"

"No. There's nothing." The mood is getting spoiled. You reach for him. "Just . . . let's just, um, not talk. At all."

"Buffy . . ." He frowns at you. "We have to be able to talk about things that are bothering us. That's part of being together."

Your mouth drops open. "*You* are saying that? You hardly ever talk! You just go all broody and silent and—"

He looks miffed. "Are you saying you don't like to be with me?"

"No!" Your temper rises. "Or maybe yes!" You stand up. "I just . . . there is nothing wrong except that I am the Slayer and you're a vampire and I bet you

don't even know that I get tired of making out in cemeteries, because after all, there is coffee, for normal
people!"

You're horrified. You didn't mean to say any of
that.

"Why are you picking a fight with me?" Angel
asks.

"Don't shout at me!" You're near tears. You have
no idea why.

You turn your back on him and begin to stomp off.

Wait. This never ends well. . . .

You whirl around.

"Angel?"

He has vanished into the night.

And you are having a very bad déjà vu experience
indeed.

*Maybe it was my guilty conscience, telling me to
go home. Maybe I should have listened.*

Maybe next time I will.

THE END

SLAYER SECOND CHANCE:
Turn to page 43.

Excuse me? Did you not get the memo about who and what you are? The Slayer? The strongest girl in all the world?

Buffy, Slayers do not flounce. *EVER.*

Puh-lese.

So you move into battle stance.

SLAYER ACTION:
Turn to page 102.

The grave slab slides back like the lid of a sardine can. Then a wizened old man with a white mustache and fuzzy sideburns wearing a pith helmet like an explorer of deepest, darkest Africa pushes back the slab and says, "Ampata, did you find it yet?"

Ampata?! That was the name of the Incan mummy princess I killed months ago. For good, I thought.

As you, Angel, the Master, and Luke stare in amazement, he takes a step up—he's on a ladder—gazes at the four of you and says to you, "You aren't Ampata! You're . . . you're that girl from the field trip! And you're vampires!"

Then he ducks back down into the grave and pulls the slab shut. Then the Master jumps on top of the grave slab and assumes battle stance!

Even counting the summer and half the new school year, you still haven't seen another vampire as gross as he looks. With his bald head and pointy ears, and his fangs and his sort-of Michael Jackson nose, you don't even know if he can attain a more human-looking appearance. Not an issue. He shouldn't even be here.

It is time to rumble, Slayer!

But from beneath the slab, you suddenly hear the old guy screaming! You glance at the stone beneath the Master's black, Nazi-like boots for half a sec, wincing at each fresh shriek.

You say to Angel, "Let's take these guys!" and jump off the slab just as the Master comes within bad breath's reach of you!

Oh, God! Does he need Mentos!

While Angel engages Luke, you shoot out your left leg in a good roundhouse kick that hits the Master smack on his evil chinny chin chin. The damage to him is one whole inch of snapback, but you take what you can get; in that moment, you reach down, grip your hands around the sides of the slab, and ram it into his chest. If he *had* any breath in his lungs, he would now be dead, or at least extremely winded.

Instead, the Master grips the edge of the slab with his long, white fingers and terrible manicure, and shoves it back at you!

Maybe someone else would stagger. But you were ready and you braced your stance for his return insult. You just give him a look as you deflect the slab by grabbing it and turning it sideways. Then you shout to Angel, who has just hit Luke in the face with a double fist, "I'm going in to check out the sitch!"

You jump straight down into the hidey-hole the slab was covering, keeping your body well away from the ladder rungs as you fall.

You hit bottom, landing squarely on your boots. Dirt clods shower the crown of your head. Brushing them away, you glance up to see Angel leaping across the hole as he takes on the Master.

You're not sure where Luke is. You so do not love leaving Angel up there alone, but there's a human being down here who has no idea who he's messing with, or what. . . .

You hear nothing. And in the darkness, you see nothing.

For all you know, Ampata is standing two inches from you, ready to suck your face!

You can't let that matter. You are the Slayer. It's your job to put your life on the line in order to save others.

You move forward into the darkness.

Above you, you hear the Master shout, "That's right, Luke! Restrain Angelus!"

There are sounds of a struggle. A terrible struggle.

The Master laughs. "Yes, my vessel. I want to have the pleasure of staking the one I had intended to sit at my right hand, and yet walked away. From me, and from his precious Darla."

"Angel, no," you whisper.

"On your knees!" Luke bellows.

The Master continues in a singsong voice. "And there was the one with the face of an angel, and he did not serve his master well. He turned away from all he knew, and all his brethren, and lived among the humans. Or tried to. And here endeth his lesson."

No! They can't kill Angel!

I have to stop them!

You start back up the ladder. Angel's feet are dangling over the hole as if he is kneeling, facing away from you.

Then you hear a scream from deep inside the earth. You stop, torn and confused.

Your duty is to protect human lives from the forces of darkness. You have seen Ampata's handiwork. You know that she can draw the life force out of a person with a single long kiss. You have seen the withered corpses of those she has killed to continue her hideous existence!

You're sure that man is as good as dead. That scream was from a distance away. You'll never be able to reach him in time. There's no long, drawn-out ritual in the way she kills.

But Angel is still alive. Well, not exactly alive, but he's about to be dusted—and you can stop it! He's your boyfriend (you hope), and there's still hope for him (you *know*) if you charge up that ladder right now and kick some Luke-and-Master vampire butt!

So what do you do, Buffy?

SLAYER CHOICE:

Do you decide to . . .

\ attempt to save Angel from the Master? *If yes, turn to page 112.*

\ accept that you must leave Angel to his fate? *If yes, turn to page 106.*

"Angel," you whisper, praying that he understands that you have to save a human being instead of him.

But you can't! You could never abandon him. Never, ever let him die!

You extend your hand as you look up, just as Angel's feet disappear from your view! There's no sound of a dusting! Rather, you hear the sound of fists slamming against a body, and you realize that Angel's still in the game!

"Angel!" you shout. "You need help?"

"I'm good!" he yells. "Go!"

Happier, and far more hopeful, you make sure you're armed, and head into the darkness to look for Ampata.

SLAYER ACTION:
Turn to page 63.

So you crouch down and put your hand around the object. It's sticky, which could mean blood or . . . other things. You can't see it, so you carry it in your left hand, saving your right for self-defense.

You leave the stench behind and wander on. Then you have another bout of dizziness. You move to the right until you find the side of the tunnel. You stay still and silent as the vertigo passes, and then you take a deep breath and prepare to move on.

But there's something behind you. You sense its presence.

You don't hear it breathing.

But you know it is evil. You can see it as surely as if it were creeping into your bones—a chilling, terrifying hatred of goodness, and life.

Of you.

You can't explain how you know this; it's just a sense. Maybe it's a slayer's special sense. You spend so much time dealing with the evil, and here it is, right behind you.

SLAYER ACTION:
Turn to page 108.

True or False?

1. Slayers are fearless Amazons who can't wait to die a valiant warrior's death.
2. Slayers never get scared.
3. Slayers never make mistakes that cost them their lives.
4. Slayers always know exactly what to do when something creeps up behind them.

Okay, Buffy, you probably got a perfect score on that. So how are you going to get 100 percent in surviving this?

SLAYER CHOICE:

Do you decide to . . .

\ turn to fight it? *If yes, turn to page 109.*

\ run like hell? *If yes, turn to page 111.*

You whirl around, extending your right arm, slicing through the air with your stake. Your knuckles are bruised with icy cold. The skin on them cracks and you jump back, grimacing with pain.

Then, realizing that your adversary will probably attack now that you've revealed yourself, you drop to the ground and sweep forward with your right leg.

There is nothing there.

Your heart is pounding; you're sweating. Your body is trying to prompt you into flight.

You stay frozen in place, forcing yourself not to pant. Your skin is prickling. Your senses are on full alert.

Something makes a whooshing sound, and then there's a sort of lumbering, staggering noise; something snaps.

It's the bone you were holding in your left hand, in the muck. Something has stepped on it and broken it.

You jerk your hand toward your chest. You contract yourself into a tight ball.

Something frozen moves right past you; its chilly evil permeates your arm and shoulder, your cheek and temple. Your eyes close in sheer terror, and you very slowly force them open again.

Remember what it was like when the Master embraced you, and you couldn't resist him? Remember the tear that slid down your cheek?

That is nothing compared to the despair and horror you feel right now. You've faced horrible things time and again, but *this* is different.

It is like a terrible virus invading your spirit.

SLAYER ACTION:
Turn to page 111.

Y ou walk forward, groping in the dark. You are so afraid.

But you feel the fear and do it anyway.

Then you hear Angel's voice calling your name.

"Here!" you nearly shout. But you keep your voice low.

You feel his hand wrapping around yours as he says, "What's wrong? You're trembling."

"I'm okay. What happened to the Master and Luke?"

"Dust in the wind," he tells you. "For now, at least."

He begins to walk you through the darkness.

"Do you know what's going on?" you ask him. "How can they come back?"

"I don't know. They thought it was nineteen thirty-seven. That's the year the earthquake trapped the Master in the underground church."

"Yeah." You nod. "All kinds of stuff has been pointing to that as some kind of . . . of . . . subject header?"

"Main topic? Focal point?"

"Yeah." You nod. And remind yourself that he's had about two hundred sixteen years longer than you to refine his vocabulary.

SLAYER ACTION:
Turn to page 116.

I will go save Angel, then save the old man, you tell yourself. *Besides, he's involved with Ampata. She won't hurt him. He knew her name and he thought she had signaled him with two stomps on the grave slab.*

But maybe she fooled him, like she fooled all of us. Or maybe he knows exactly what she is and he's supplying her with victims. A man like that doesn't deserve to live.

But those aren't the kind of calls you're allowed to make, Buffy. You don't get to decide who lives and who dies in the human realm. You're the Vampire Slayer, not the judge, jury, and executioner of the human race. You're not some kind of vigilante. You have a sacred duty . . . which you are now considering abandoning.

But don't you get points for saving your soul mate?

You'll have to see if the universe punishes you . . . and if you can live with yourself . . . as you race up the ladder and see Angel's feet dangling over the edge.

Without warning, you grab his ankles and pull down at an angle as you leap off the ladder and back down into the darkness. Gravity does the rest as Angel drops down too, landing on top of you and pushing your face into the dirt in a position that probably has an extremely cool name in yoga. However, in your world, it's called Butt in the Air, Boyfriend Crushing Upper Back. You're actually surprised he didn't break your back when you broke his fall.

You're stunned for a moment, regrouping as he

rises up and straddles your shoulders, then walks on his knees around your head. Springing to his feet, he turns and grips your wrists, as you spring to a standing position.

"Thanks," he says. "You good?"

"You're welcome. I'm fine."

Then Luke drops down, wedged between you and the ladder like a playing card in a deck inside the box.

All he has to do is open his mouth and he can rip out the back of your neck!

So you jab your elbows backward as hard as you can. Then you shout, "Angel!" and drop to a crouch as Angel pummels him, totally battering him like when Giles holds a punching bag and shouts, "Again, again!" like a crazed Teletubby—which is this insane TV show about a group of stuffed creatures Xander showed you on a bootleg from Australia. It will never make it in the States.

So he gives Luke the one-two-three-four-five-six while Luke starts trying to kick you. But you sit down on his feet while you reach up and over your shoulder and work on the nearest rung of the ladder. Finally it gives way, and you say, "Angel, stake!" and pass it up to him. He pauses in his punching-bag routine long enough to take it from you and stab Luke in the heart with it!

Happy New Year! It's like confetti, only it's vampire dust!

You hear the Master aboveground howling with fury. You see Angel's look of satisfaction in the dim moonlight.

Then the Master shouts, "What are you doing here? You'll pay for intruding on my sorrow!"

There's an answering cry.

"Angel, someone's up there," you say. "We have to go save them!"

You turn to go. "Buffy, wait," Angel urges you. "Go slow. We don't know what's going on up there."

But there's another shout.

SLAYER CHOICE:

Do you decide to . . .

❚ rush back to the surface to investigate because someone up there may need your help? *If yes, turn to page 115.*

❚ go for the surer thing—a man in danger here in the tunnels? Do you take Angel's hand and run into the darkness? *If yes, turn to page 116.*

"**N**o, Buffy—wait!" Angel cries as you race back up the ladder.

You pop out of the hole . . . only to find the Master standing over one of his own vampire minions, who is kneeling with his head down. The Master is brandishing a stake over his head and speaking to him.

"Luke was twice the vampire you are, and yet you dare to smirk when you see that I have lost him," he is saying to the minion, and then he sees you. His beady eyes glitter, and he grins as he leaps straight at you.

You try to jump back down the hole, but the Master is on you! He slams the stake into your chest. The pain is agonizing.

As you go into shock, he leers at you. Then he sinks his fangs into you. You remember the first time he did this. You've never been able to forget it.

Angel will come, you tell yourself.

But the world begins to blur as the Master sucks the life out of you. You can hear your own heart, and it is slowing.

He whispers in your ear, "You gave up your life to save a vampire, Slayer. Don't you find the irony delicious?"

Not so much, you think.

And then you think of nothing at all. . . .

THE END

Now, happily, you can move faster than you would have if you'd let Angel get killed. Because vampires can see in the dark!

So you and Angel haul; he says, "We're in a maze of tunnels. To the left I can smell somebody who's really afraid, and I smell blood to the right," he tells you. "But it smells weird. Like something's wrong with it."

"Is it human blood? Living?"

"I don't know. It's really . . . off."

Okay, Slayer, which way do you go? How do you decide?

You can almost hear Giles saying, "This is called *triage*, Buffy. When you, as the Slayer, must decide how best to save two different people who both need your aid."

You could use more time to ponder the meaning of that, because you know there is something in France called the Arc de Triage—the Arch of Triage? However, the French are strange. They also have a flag that's red, white, and blue, which has nothing to do with colonies, and you've learned to deal. You've also learned that a wandering mind is a terrible thing to use for slaying, so you make a command decision.

SLAYER CHOICE:

Do you decide to . . .

❧ go left toward the fear? *If yes, turn to page 117.*

❧ go right toward the blood? *If yes, turn to page 126.*

"We need to go left," you tell Angel. "Fear means someone living, for sure. I gotta protect the living." You hold tight to his hand—what a chore—and say, "Let's kick it!"

You and Angel start running. Lucky thing you're the Slayer, because Angel has long legs and he knows how to use them. Plus, he can run for a long time. Preternatural vampire strength means preternatural stamina. That statement would have Xander twitching and saying something like, "Don't talk about his stamina! His stamina is not something we discuss!"

But Xander is not here. Which is to the good. Because while Xander is quick with the comeback, you now need to be quick with the footsteps.

"The blood is a lot closer, Buffy," Angel says. "I can't be sure, but I think someone's seriously injured."

"You think we should check? Is it really close?"

"It's your call. But yes, it's very close."

SLAYER CHOICE:

Do you decide to . . .

\ make a quick detour and check out the blood? *If yes, turn to page 237.*

\ stay on course for the fear? *If yes, turn to page 118.*

Yatou are not prepared for what you see. Because first of all, you are underground, and yet you *can* see. There are torches set into the walls. The old man with the white mustache is kneeling over the dusty, caved-in body of Ampata, the Inca mummy princess. His pith helmet is pressed to his chest, and he is silently weeping.

You slow your speed and walk gingerly up to him. You put your hand on his shoulder so as not to startle him.

He looks up at you and says, "I knew what she was. I dared defy her gods, because I was too greedy."

"What do you mean?" you ask him. He looks vaguely familiar, but you can't place him.

"You don't remember me? I'm Carey Koneff," he says, looking up at you. "I was the one who led your class tour of Ampata's tomb at the museum. After that kid broke that plate, she rose up out of her sarcophagus and tried to kill me! But I grabbed the emergency fire ax and held her off!"

"Oh, I do remember you," you tell him. "In fact, I was just thinking about you the other day. I wondered if anyone in the museum saw her leave her tomb. I wondered if you did."

"I did." He lowers his head. "She told me that she had heard something about Sunnydale when she was on exhibit in New York. A curator there was telling a colleague that there's supposed to be a fabulous treasure buried underneath the town. In the school basement. She made a deal with me. She promised me that if I'd help her stay alive, she'd show me the treasure."

You look at him. You are very confused, because this doesn't match up with the way it happened. Plus, you killed Ampata. Months ago.

"You would find victims for her?" you verify. When he nods, you ask, "Did you send her to the bus station to kill my foreign exchange student?"

"It doesn't matter now," he replies, avoiding your piercing Slayer gaze. "She lied to me. She said there was a treasure there, which was buried by the school principal in nineteen thirty-seven . . . but there isn't. I searched there a few hours ago. And nothing is there."

He starts to cry. "I let her do this to me for nothing!"

"What are you talking about?" you ask him. "You're alive."

"Yes, but I'm only twenty-nine!" he cries out. "When I couldn't find her someone fast enough, I had to let her inhale some of my life force, a little at a time. And now . . . I feel so sick. I think I'm dying."

Then his eyes widen and he whispers in a strangled voice, *"Ampata?"*

You turn. The beautiful young girl gazes at you and Angel, and says, "Dr. Koneff, you promised to bring me someone young and filled with life, and so you have."

"How can you be back?" the man asks querulously. He points to the corpse on the ground. "I killed you myself, not two minutes ago!"

Ampata ignores him as she opens her arms and advances on Angel.

Just then, the ground beneath your feet shifts and shakes. Rocks and chunks of dirt plummet from overhead.

The ground shakes again.

Angel says, "Buffy, get him out of here!"

Then a large rock shakes loose and hits Angel on the head. Stunned, he drops to his knees.

Ampata lunges at him, grabbing his shoulders, and leans down toward him.

"No!" Dr. Koneff shouts. "Don't let her kiss you. she'll kill you!"

The ground shakes a third time; you grab Dr. Koneff's left arm and say, "C'mon, I'm going to get you out of here."

He resists, pointing a shaking finger toward Ampata and Angel, locked in an embrace.

"It's okay," you tell Dr. Koneff. "Angel is a vampire. He doesn't have any life force for her to suck out . . ." *Whoops.*

Ampata says to Angel, "You are useless!" Then she grabs a stake from his jacket pocket and aims it straight at his heart!

The ground shakes harder. More debris tumbles down; you attempt to shield Dr. Koneff as Ampata continues to grapple with Angel. She is amazingly strong.

SLAYER CHOICE:

Do you decide to . . .

❚ get Dr. Koneff out of the tunnel? *If yes, turn to page 122.*

❚ attempt to save Angel first? *If yes, turn to page 124.*

This time, you know you must save this man. Your first priority as a slayer must be to preserve human life.

The ground is rocking, and the tunnel might collapse at any moment as you half-drag, half-carry Dr. Koneff back the way you and Angel came, hoping that you have taken all the correct twists and turns.

You frantically start to push him up the ladder before you remember that the Master might still be up there. So you go first, poking your head out.

There is no sign of him.

Dr. Koneff says, "I'm getting out of here!"

"Wait," you order. "I need to make sure you're safe."

"My car is over there," he tells you. He points to a black Volvo station wagon parked across the street.

You take his hand and run with him through the cemetery gates, muttering, "C'mon, c'mon!" as he fumbles with the lock in the car door.

Then he's in. He starts the engine and peels out, the wheels squealing.

You race back in the cemetery and down the ladder and into the tunnel. The ground is shaking. You shout, "Angel!"

You reach the cavern with the torches, to find Angel looking totally fine as he is standing over Ampata—or rather, what you assume is Ampata, because there are chunks of what appears to be freeze-dried leather all over the cavern. Then you see her dried-up head . . . ew . . .

You run to him and say, "I was afraid she was going to kill you."

He shakes his head. "She had the power to inflict damage on me, just like when the rock hit me, but I'm still immortal."

You're so glad. You give him a kiss, and then the ground shakes again. Angel says, "We have to get out of here. Go straight, and then go left, remember?"

SLAYER ACTION:
Turn to page 126.

"**A**ngel!" you cry, leaving Dr. Koneff to fend for himself.

You run up behind Ampata, grab her by the shoulders, and yank hard. As before, her arms rip from her torso and thump to the ground, and she mummifies in your grasp.

You fall backward.

The cavern begins to shake really, really hard. You struggle to rise, then see that a huge cascade of dirt has collapsed on Dr. Koneff. He is buried.

"Angel!" you shout as you get to your feet. He is across the cavern. You have been thrown across the floor by the earthquake.

As you attempt to dig Dr. Koneff out of the rubble, the ground ripples and vibrates; then the head of an enormous, snakelike creature bursts through the ground beside you. It is shimmering with gems, and it has an elongated head like a Chinese dragon and a fluted, webbed back and huge leathery wings.

It opens its mouth wide. Huge fangs glisten and gleam; mucus—of course!—ropes from two enormous incisors. Its jaws open wide, then snap shut.

You are suddenly flooded with a terrible despair. Tears spring to your eyes as you prepare to fight the monster. It's doing this to you, but you don't know how to stop the rush of sorrow.

Then you see Dr. Koneff's fingers poke through the dirt. They wiggle, then go slack.

As you start to dig Dr. Koneff out, the creature rises up to the top of the cavern and hangs there, facing you, preparing to strike.

My priority should have been saving Dr. Koneff. If I had done that, this wouldn't be happening.

The creature opens its huge mouth. Flame erupts in a stream, hurtling straight for you.

You spare a thought for your successor, who will become the Chosen One after your death.

You hope that she is better prepared for her role than you were.

Then a fiery cloud of death envelopes you.

THE END

As you turn to the left, the ground rumbles and shakes. You're thrown off your feet, colliding with Angel as you both tumble to the earth!

Dirt and rocks cascade from above you. It's like a waterfall of dirt—a dirtfall!—and you cover your head and take a breath, bending forward in hopes of creating an air pocket for yourself.

The dirtfall buries you. You hold your breath.

Then you remember something that gives you hope.

Something about vampires.

About Angel.

Angel doesn't have to breathe! His lungs don't work.

The hills are alive, and so are you, in the tunnel, as he digs you out. Okay, so he couldn't give you CPR when the Master once drowned you, but this is the second time that his no need of breath has saved you and/or your friends.

You can't see anything, but his fingers find your face and he holds you close for a moment before he says, "We have to get out of here, Buffy. Whatever caused that cave-in might happen again."

"I think it was an earthquake," you tell him as you wipe the dirt from your eyes. You can see him in the moonlight that's gleaming through a hole that the quake created. You wonder if the Master and Luke are still up there waiting.

"Yeah, Sunnydale has endured some bad ones," he says. "Of course, the worst one was in nineteen thirty-seven."

"The one that trapped the Master. Angel, what's going on?"

He shakes his head. "I don't know. Maybe Giles can figure it out."

"I hope so," you say sincerely.

You two reach the surface and cautiously look around. Car alarms are wailing in the distance. Dogs are barking. You hear a siren. Then another.

You sigh. "Another typical Monday night." You stride over to the hole with the ladder, which is still intact. "I should probably go see if there's anything else down there."

"No. Go home," Angel says. "I'll go back down and see if I can find whoever it is. You know there could be aftershocks. I won't suffocate."

"It's my job," you insist.

He shakes his head. "It's unnecessary. Giles would tell you the same thing."

You're not too happy about it, but he's right: Sometimes you have to know when to throw in the towel. Which is not the same as running like hell.

"All right." You sigh.

Then he puts his arms around you and kisses you. Mudface meets mudface, but it feels so good. And hey, no barfy dizziness this time!

"Be careful."

"I will. You too," you tell him.

You watch him over your shoulder as you walk back through the cemetery. Angel descends the ladder.

Lights are on in your neighborhood as you walk

toward your house, which looks just fine.

You see a familiar silhouette waiting at your front steps. It's Xander.

"Buffy!" Xander calls. Then, seeing your "shush" gestures, he lowers his voice and heads toward you.

"You are so much the Slayer I want to see," he tells you. "What's going on?"

The phone inside starts ringing. You let yourself and Xander into the house, race into the kitchen, and grab it.

"Honey?" your mom says on the other end. "Are you all right?"

"Yes, I'm fine," you assure her. "Wow, that was some earthquake, wasn't it?"

She sighs. "They're so much worse here than they ever were in L.A. Who knew? Of course our helpful real estate woman never mentioned that. At least I bought quake insurance. I hope our foundation didn't crack. It's cement, but—"

"Mom," you interrupt gently. "When are you coming home? It's late. I didn't even know you'd left," you add guiltily. You snuck out of the window as usual.

"I had to check on something at the gallery. I knocked on your door to see if you wanted to come. It's very exciting."

"Oh?" You look at Xander. "Something exciting? *What* exciting?"

"I'll tell you when I get home. I just have to lock up."

"Okay. I'll be waiting for you." You hang up.

You say to Xander, "I have to take a shower. Fast! My mom thinks I've been asleep for hours!"

"Okay!" Xander cries. "Let's go!" He blushes. "I mean, I'll go!"

"Thanks. But what did you want?" you ask.

He shrugs. "I was going home from Willow's—she's still trying to save my butt in math, my math butt—and I started thinking about how I always end up with these weird demon girlfriends. Like Ampata and Miss French. Who, okay, was not exactly my girlfriend, but . . ."

You're all ears. Dirty ears, whose mom is on her way home, but still ears. Which, wait a minute . . . is your mom the mom of your ears?

"You were thinking about Ampata?" you ask Xander.

"Yeah, and then I felt really dizzy. And kind of vomitous." He frowns at you. "Do I have a fever?"

You feel his forehead. "No."

"Well, it's gone now. Maybe it was something I ate. The Rosenbergs offered me some herring." He shudders. "You go that route, next thing you know, you're eating schwarma."

He leaves via the kitchen door, giving you a wave.

You go up and shower.

You are clean and you smell like a girl again as your mother comes into the house, calling, "Buffy! I'm home!"

"Thank God! I mean, good, hi!" you say as you

greet her at the top of the stairs. "How'd it go?"

"Fine, except that I think I might be coming down with something," she says. She puts a hand to her head and adds, "Or maybe it was something I ate."

"I'm sorry," you say sincerely.

"I didn't sleep well," she continues. "I had a nightmare." She makes a face. "About Ted."

"He was no good, Mom," you say wryly.

She appreciates your humor. "Not to worry, honey. I'm dating mummies now." She grins at your look of shock. "Actually, I'm just making labels for some beautiful pieces we just got in. They're copies of Egyptian funereal jewelry. They were worn by mummies of different time periods."

"Egyptian, not Incan?" you ask.

"No." Your mom smiles at you. "And I have to confess that I'm impressed that you know the Incans had mummies.

SLAYER ACTION:
Turn to page 131.

"**W**ell. I do. But what were you so excited about?"
you ask.

"Oh." Your mom's face just lights up. "We got the
most amazing thing today. I have an intern from U.C.
Sunnydale. George Handley. You'd like him. Although
he's too old for you."

"Mom."

"George has been researching the earthquake of
nineteen thirty-seven. And today he unearthed a time
capsule from that very year! It was in the high school
basement. Principal Snyder didn't want to let us have
it, but George's aunt is on the school board. So, we
have it!"

Nineteen thirty-seven? Could things be yet weirder?

"What's in it?" you ask, trying to sound calm.

Joyce raises her brows. "It's a mystery. We haven't
opened it yet. The key is missing, and we don't want to
force the lock."

"Where, missing?" you ask. "Who has it?"

You two have reached her bedroom door. As she
opens it, she says, "Well, if we knew where it was, it
wouldn't be missing, would it?" She moves her shoulders. "It's quite a mystery, isn't it?"

"Sure is." You smile at her.

"We're going to ask some older alumni, see if anyone knows where it might be. Unfortunately, there
aren't a lot of alumni left. Well, good night, Buffy."

"Night, Mom."

She shuts the door . . .

. . . leaving you to stare at it while your mind

churns. You have a feeling that the key is the key to the mystery of what's going on. In other words, the key is *key*.

Jeesh, the way you think sometimes, someone would think you get paid by the word. . . .

But you get results with action. So you wait a decent amount of time for her to go to sleep and head for the scene of the mystery.

SLAYER ACTION:
Turn to page 133.

Here you are at your mom's gallery. It's got a dark wood exterior, and the sign over the door reads SUNNY-DALE GALLERY. Short and to the point. It is a thing of pride with you that Joyce did such an awesome job of starting over. Mom power.

There's a light on. You creep over to the window and peek inside. You see masks and statues, none of which are either glowing or moving. Lots of windows you could break, locks to destroy. But *aha!* Before you left the house, you snagged the extra key your mom keeps in the cupboard next to the sugar substitute.

You jog around to the back, crossing your fingers that the key fits that lock—you're back in the all-black look, and no matter how casual you want to appear, it's after midnight and you have a very lame excuse prepared in case you're stopped by a police officer. And if he/she/they call your mom, you are dead.

Yes! The back door unlocks, and you sneak in.

You look around. Lots of pottery. And little statues. Ooh, jewelry.

Then you hear a noise in the back room. There's a coffee machine, a desktop PC, and a little refrigerator in there, for breaks and office work. You tiptoe toward it, stake at the ready.

But nothing is there.

Then something leaps at you!

SLAYER ACTION:
Turn to page 134.

ait!

It's a cat!

It's a regular cat, not a zombie cat, nothing weird. It's part Siamese, and it looks up at you and says, "Mrrrow."

Then the back door opens wide!

"There you are!" someone calls.

Footsteps.

You whirl around.

Oh.

My.

God.

A truly amazing guy walks toward you. He has blond hair and blue eyes, and he's six foot *hot*. He smiles, cocks his head, and says, "Buffy?"

"Um, hello," you say cautiously. "My mom . . . forgot something, and I came to get it. Even though it's very late."

"Me too. I forgot my cat!" He laughs. It's a good laugh. "I forgot I brought her down today. Our frat house is being tented for termites, so I had to bring her in."

You are staring at him. He says, "Where are my manners? I'm George Handley. I'm an art history intern—"

"From U.C. Sunnydale," you finish for him. "Hi. I'm . . . well, you know who I am. And I am who that is."

The cat sidles up to him and starts rubbing her side

back and forth against the calf of his right leg. You can hear her purring.

With a dimply grin, he bends down and picks her up. "So, what did your mom forget?" he asks you.

You blink. "What? Oh. Um." You smile. "Actually, it was something I told her I had already gotten for her. Then I realized I'd forgotten it too, ha-ha. So she doesn't know I'm here in the middle of the night to get . . . that which we both forgot."

He pets the cat. "Covering your tracks. I get that." He motions zipping his mouth and throwing away the key. "Don't worry. Your secret is safe with me."

Oh God, I hope so.

"So," you say, "she was telling me about the time capsule. How did you find it?"

He blinks at you and stops petting the cat. "Oh, I'm doing a double major in art and archaeology, and there are so many fascinating finds here in Sunnydale. Come and see."

He walks over to a large wooden box and takes off the lid with a flourish. Then he looks in, and his smile disappears. "It's gone!" he shouts. "It's been stolen! We have to call the police!"

"Oh. We." Your voice quavers. How are you going to explain this to your mom if she finds you here?

"Could you let me leave first?" you ask him weakly. "I would really be in so much trouble if my mom found out I, uh, am not home. . . ."

He hesitates. "You didn't take it? Like a school prank, or some kind of sorority initiation—"

"No, no, I promise," you say, beginning to actually cross your heart, then realizing that that is so childish, and this guy is in college.

"Okay," he says slowly. "I probably shouldn't, but hey, it's okay."

"Thanks." You sag with relief. And hightail it to the back door. You open it, wonder if there's going to be a problem with fingerprints, and then leave.

You're halfway back around the building when you realize that you left your mom's key in the break room! You set it down when the cat startled you.

You double back.

George is on the phone. Calling the police, you assume.

Then you see a shape darting around the other side of the building.

You run past the back door and follow it.

It's Ethan Rayne! And he's carrying a silver canister under his arm!

You silently race after him. But as you pursue him, he turns around and waves his hands.

A strange blue light shimmers around him.

The light glitters and blossoms. Then he stares right at you and waves. The blue light vanishes, and he's gone.

You feel violently ill, and filled with a terrible dread.

You're nearly paralyzed with fear. You tremble from head to toe.

You have to shut your eyes tightly and press your knuckles against your mouth to keep from throwing up. Tears and sweat trail down your temples.

Just then, a police car arrives. A flashlight beam glows near where you're standing. You duck behind a trash can.

After a few minutes, another police car pulls up to the curb. Its lights are flashing.

Ethan is long gone.

You realize that George will probably call your mom to tell her about the theft. You would really like to run to Giles's place and tell him about all this, but you'd better cover your tracks by getting home as fast as you can.

If you can even stand . . . .

You watch the police officers go inside the art gallery. They'll start searching the grounds.

It's now or not.

You take off, racing home. You climb in bed just as your mom opens the door. She says, "Buffy? Are you awake?"

"Oh, huh? Hi, Mom."

"Something terrible has happened!" she tells you. "The gallery's been broken into and someone stole our time capsule!"

Yeah, and I know who, you want to tell her. You say, "That's terrible, Mom."

She's distracted. You can see by the light in the hallway that she's thrown on some sweatpants and a jacket. "Well, I have to go down there. You stay here. I'll be back as soon as I can."

"Okay." You hope George really can keep your secret.

As soon as your mom is gone, you sit up and dial Giles.

His phone rings and rings. There is no answer. Maybe he's at the library.

You think about racing over there, but that's too dicey. Your mom might find out you've left. But you have to do something!

So you call Willow.

"Buffy?" she says after the first ring. Of course Will has caller ID. She's totally jacked in. "So, did you find Giles? What did he say about Ethan Rayne?"

You blink. "Huh?"

"And how did you get home so fast?"

You say again, "Huh?"

"Are you all right?" she asks.

"I'm just confused," you tell her. "I . . . what about Ethan Rayne?"

"Well, I don't know," Willow replies. "You just called me. I thought you were coming over here."

You are baffled.

Then a dark shape enters your window!

You whirl around with the phone in your hand.

It's Spike! Spike is in your bedroom!

"Slayer!" he says gleefully as he lands on top of

your bedspread. *With dirty boots!* He gives you a once-over and says, "You look good enough to kill."

"Buffy?" Willow shouts in the phone. "What's going on?"

SLAYER ACTION:
Turn to page 153.

You throw down the phone. Then you throw down with Spike. As he comes at you, you execute a round-house that connects hard with his hip. He flies backward. You lunge at him. "Get out of my bedroom!" you shout at him. "You're not even real! You're a fake!"

"Wrong, Slayer. I'm as real as they come. I'm your death, wearin' a great coat! Which I took off a dead slayer—one of two I've killed."

Then he tears at you, fully vamped, and he is wild!

You trade blows as he shouts at you, "Can't resist, can you! You are the most arrogant, brainless bint I've ever come across! I'll tear you to bits before I allow you to speak like that to me again! No one smears Manchester United and lives!"

What?

You are totally, thoroughly confused. You were holding your own in the hit parade, but now you feel off-balance and unsure. Blood is dripping from a gash over your eye, and you shake your head to keep it out of your eyes.

Spike sniffs. He tilts his head and says, "Something wrong with you? You smell off. Not that that'll keep me from rippin' your head off!"

Then he slams you hard against the wall. You are stunned.

You can hear the metallic crackle of shouting on the other end of the portable phone as Spike bends down and grabs it without taking his eyes off you.

"Whoever this is, I'm about to kill the Slayer! She'll be my third. It's a personal best . . . Slayer? What are you . . . ?" He gazes at you and says into the phone, "What are you doin' in two places at once?"

Two places at once? There must be a double of you! And it's at Willow's house!

"Willow!" you shout. "It's a fake Buffy!"

"What's that?" Spike grins at you. "Oh, hi, *Buffy*," he says into the phone. Then he turns his attention to you. "Slayer is sayin' *you're* the fake!"

He throws the phone at you and hits you, hard. Then he closes both hands around your throat and throws you to the bed. He straddles you and begins to choke the life out of you.

You see a stake on the bed stand. You reach for it as the world smears to gray. There's a buzzing in your head. You can't see anything but his leering face. You stretch out your hand, fumbling, losing consciousness.

Then your hand closes around it! You lift it up, preparing to impale him.

"Go on!" he says, laughing. Then you feel it wrenched out of your hand.

And your entire chest bursts into pain. He's staked you! You feel your blood gushing from your chest!

The world is going black!

YOU ARE DYING!

The room is bathed in a strange blue glow. Everything shimmers.

Then, you sense movement at the window. You glance over and find a strangely misshapen gargoyle-like hulk gazing at you. It looks like a mutant frog, and it is sitting on the sill. Its large belly is glowing with that eerie blue light; and some deep-seated, primeval part of you is screaming for you to run away from it.

Standing beside it—in the tree?—another extremely ugly creature leers at you. His face is a death mask, and enjoying your pain. Maybe at one point it was a person, but it is even less human-looking than the Master. It has black holes for eyes, and purplish-green skin pulled over a skull. Horns protrude from its head and curl into ultra-sharp points. It's wearing a black robe spangled with stars and moons.

And it is smiling as it watches you struggle.

As it watches you dying.

"Who the bloody hell are you two?" Spike demands.

It opens its mouth and says, "I am Lars Von Teufelsblut. Lars Devils' Blood, in your language. Ethan Rayne has asked me for my services. And in return . . . I will see my one true love again."

"But you, you are nothing. You are an apparition. A memory. A joke. And very soon, *mein Schatz,* you will cease to exist."

"You're out of your mind, mate," Spike says, crossing to the window. "That there is a genuine Vampire Slayer, she's dying, and I'm the one done her in!"

As he rushes the two figures, everything fades and

blurs. You can't hear Spike's voice anymore. You can't hear anything.

I'm not dying. And I'm not fake! you think desperately. *I'm not!*

I'm me.

I'm . . .

SLAYER ACTION:
Turn to page 31.

You and Willow finally found Giles here at the library. It's five in the morning, and you are thoroughly wigged as you recount what you heard over the phone at Willow's house. Which was you, dying.

Killed by Spike.

"The doubling must have occurred when Ethan caused that blue shimmering field," Giles muses.

"And the real me came here looking for you because you were also not home," you say indignantly.

"Well, pardon me for having a Black and Tan at the Lucky Pint while I did my research," he says.

"Beer is bad," you say. "And did you drink all night? Eww, I don't want to know if you picked up some-some chippie."

"Chippie?" he repeats. "Great merciful heavens, where did you learn to talk like that?"

You look hurt. And wonder if "chippie" is a nasty word, when you just thought it meant skanky English ho.

"So I waited for you, and while I was waiting, I called Willow. And then I decided to go over to her house."

"And that was when your double called her." Giles nodded. "It's very eerie, don't you think?"

"No, I don't think. I know. Willow knows also."

"Yes. Very wiggy," Willow agrees. She looks very tired and frightened.

You cross your arms over your chest. "I guess Spike killed me." You look very unhappy. "And we thought Spike was dead because we killed him in the church fire."

"He is. Or very well may be. I'm working on my time warp theory. It keeps coming back to nineteen thirty-seven. Now, you saw Ethan Rayne steal the time capsule last night at the gallery."

"I did," you assert. "I told Willow about it. Right before . . . the doubling thing." You are still wigged.

Giles considers. "Perhaps he's helping the Master return to the time he attempted to open the Hellmouth. That would explain all the doubles, and the earthquake as well."

"Why?" you ask. "We weren't alive in nineteen thirty-seven."

"Maybe he hasn't got it calibrated correctly," Willow ventures. "He's making a lot of bungled attempts. He hasn't gotten it right yet."

"Maybe the time capsule was the missing ingredient in getting it right," Willow continues. "And now he has it."

"No joy there," you say glumly.

Giles opens up the can of stinky mound stuff that you retrieved for him from the basement a few minutes ago.

"Willow, you'll start examining it, yes?"

She makes a face. Then she opens up her little Velma forensics bag and starts pulling on a pair of latex gloves.

Giles starts moving around the library, picking up books and examining them, and putting them back down. "We'll work until school starts," he says.

"I have to be in Snyder's office before first period,"

you remind him. "I'm supposed to read my textbooks."
You smirk at the very idea.

"Excellent." Giles hefts one of his dusty books and
hands it to you. "Read this. We'll put a Sunnydale
High School book cover on it, and he'll never know the
difference." He mutters to himself, "I sincerely doubt
that man knows *how* to read."

You look down at the book. "*Ectoplasms, Muci,
and Demonic Excretions*?" you read off the cover,
which shows a horned demon with a very, very big
nose. "You're kidding."

"I assure you, I am not," he tells you. "These
stinky mounds"—he points to Willow's specimen—
"I'm sure they're demonic excretions of some sort. If
we can figure out what creature is extruding them,
we'll be that much closer to figuring out what Ethan is
about. Willow, have you an extra book cover?"

"Sure do," she says cheerily.

"Right." He says to you, "Begin reading whatever
it is you usually read in his office, then make the
switch when he's not looking."

"Okay," you say unhappily.

SLAYER ACTION:
Turn to page 8.

Y ou stare at a picture of . . . ewww, what is the obsession here with mucus?

Tick, tock, tick, tock.

Your head is lolling, and your eyes are closing. . . .

Tick, tock, tick, tock . . .

Didn't you already read this page?

You don't know how you do it, but you get through the hour of reading the demon mucus book. Then you get through school. Wow, attending classes gives you a whole different perspective on the learning.

Then, as Giles requested, you return to the library.

"Very good," he says as you come in. "I really think we're getting somewhere. As I thought, that odd material was mucus. The mucus of a Shimera demon. They are absolutely beautiful. Covered with gold and precious stones."

"Why does it not surprise me that Ethan Rayne would be interested in such a thing?" you say dryly.

"Indeed."

"Willow and Xander should be here in a bit. Meanwhile, I have another book for you to read."

"Book?" you say as Giles leads you to the big, fat, enormous *Book of Thoth* on the study table. "I am not research girl. I am the Slayer. You are the Watcher. You do the reading!"

He flips open the book. "I think I'm onto something here, but we need to move as quickly as we can. I'm not feeling well, and Ms. Caulfield has assured me that there really is a stomach virus going round."

"It's probably just food poisoning," you grumble.

"You British people and the weird food. You probably ate schwarma for breakfast."

"Baked beans and toast," he says, looking affronted.

"And yet," you murmur.

He turns to a page. "Nevertheless, it surely must have occurred to you before this that I might become ill, or hurt, or even die." He pushes up his glasses. "What would you do then, I ask you?"

"I'd ask Willow to read the big, dusty books," you say, with the thrust-forward bottom lip. It still doesn't work. "Willow loves the knowledge!"

He crosses his arms. "What if she is sick or incapacitated?"

"Don't say what if Willow dies!" you cry, stricken. "Willow can't die!"

"Oh, God," says a voice from the library doorway.

You and Giles turn. It's Oz, the black-nailed guitarist who likes Willow. He looks terrible.

"Oh! H-hi," you say, sounding all like you have something to hide.

"Hello. May I help you?" Giles asks, far more neutral. Like he's asking him, "Would you like a cup of coffee?"

"Willow . . . ?" Oz looks like he's about to vomit. "Willow is *dying*?"

"No! She's fine, fine!" you assure him. "We were discussing a—"

"Hypothetical situation," Giles fills in for you. Thank God, he with the long words. "Having nothing, actually, to do with Willow."

"We just mentioned her name by accident," you assure Oz.

"Yes," Giles says, backing you up.

Oz looks wary.

You nod vigorously. "Hypothetical, and not about her. She's fine. Really."

Oz exhales. Some color comes back to his cheeks. You are touched. You also wonder if Willow knows this guy is attracted.

"Okay, then." Oz pauses, looking at the two of you. "I was here to check something out."

"Ah. A book?" Giles asks, all excited.

"Yes, actually."

"To read?" Giles is about to just faint.

"Not exactly. On guitar fingering," Oz says kindly, letting him down easy. Oz walks a little cautiously into the library proper. "I'm working on my E-flat, diminished ninth."

"Indeed." Giles's eyes widen with admiration and maybe some wistfulness. "A man's chord." He smiles faintly. "One could lose a finger."

You clear your throat. Giles comes back to reality and says, "Well, yes. We have a number of books on the guitar. Also, some articles in various . . . places. I've been trying to subscribe to a few guitar magazines, or even one, but the library budget being what it is . . ."

Oz wanders over to the study table and glances down at Giles's big, dusty book. The one he wants you to do research in. "*The Book of Thoth*?" he says. "Looks . . . expensive."

"Well, looks can be deceiving," you say quickly, moving between Oz and the book. "After all, Cordelia looks expensive, and she's . . ." You are not going there. "Don't judge a book by its cover," you add, smiling anxiously at your Watcher. "Right, Giles?"

"Quite right." Giles goes into hustle mode as he frantically looks through the stacks. "Ah! Here we are!" He pulls out a book and hands it to Oz.

"Thanks." Oz glances down at it, then at Giles. "Don't I have to, like, check it out of the library or something?"

"No," Giles says quickly. "Honor system." He smiles blankly. "This week only. An experiment."

"Cool." Oz turns to go.

"Hey." You rush up to him. You *so* want him and Willow to get together. "She likes animal crackers." You nod eagerly as he takes this information in. "The kind in the little boxes that look like circus wagons."

There is actually a faint blush of pink on his cheeks as he regards you with a lazy smile. He says, "Thanks."

Then Oz leaves.

"Now, we shall read," Giles announces.

Read.

Read.

Read-y, read-y, read.

Then Giles says, "I've been thinking about something, Buffy. Spike attacked you in your home, yes?"

"Yes. I guess my double must have invited him in. Stupid double."

Giles continues to read.

"I should train," you say. "I need to stay in shape if I'm going to be fighting all the bad guys twice."

Giles shakes his head. "You were up all night, and you've put in a full school day. There are times when one ought to conserve one's strength."

"Yeah, if you're really old . . . I mean, not sixteen," you shoot back.

SLAYER ACTION:
Turn to page 155.

But your question is never answered . . . because Spike and Dru drop down from the ceiling!

"Slayer!" Spike cries with delight as he lands solidly on his feet like a big black cat. He's all vamped out; with his light blond hair and sharp features, he looks like Billy Idol gone terribly wrong. He's wearing that long black coat and his steel-toed boots. "Fancy meetin' you here! Let's have a dance, then, eh?"

"We'll have a party," Dru coos. "With cakes. And brandied pears." She wafts toward Giles and growls at him, wriggling her long, crescent-moon fingernails. "Bad doggy," she adds as Giles grabs a cross off the study table and holds it in front of himself. "Spike, make him put that down."

"I will, poodle," Spike says, without taking his eyes off you. "Soon as I take care of the Slayer."

"Yeah, right," you say. "I'm going to wipe the floor with your coat."

Spike frowns at you. "First rule of combat, Slayer: Never touch the coat."

He launches himself at you.

SLAYER ACTION:
Turn to page 153.

Your Slayer senses ratchet up to red alert. You know Spike's style: He has no style. Spike acts first and thinks . . . never. He's all about being impulsive.

You back up far enough so that when he lands, he's still too far away to grab you. You back up again.

SLAYER ACTION:

If you're in the bedroom on the phone with Willow, turn to page 140.

If you're in the library with Giles, turn to page 154.

"You can kill my double, but you can't kill me!"
you shout at him.

He frowns. "What the hell you goin' on about?"

"Mirrors, and smoke!" Dru coos.

Okay, so this Spike isn't the same Spike that killed
your double. You don't even want to think about that.
You don't have time to think about that. Spike is one of
your fiercest enemies. Now is the time to kick his butt.
For real.

Spike is really strong. He is forcing you away,
putting space between you and Giles while Drusilla
wags her fingers at Giles and giggles. Or maybe she's
growling some more. She is so supremely weird. . . .

Spike hits you really hard. You hit him back really
hard.

Now . . . did you listen to Giles? Did you briefly
rest? Or did you just have to do the training?

SLAYER ACTION:

If you did the step routine, turn to page 157.

If you started on your nails, turn to page 164.

"**I** am your Watcher, Buffy," Giles reminds you. "I do have some experience in these matters. And I don't recommend a training session at this point."

"Giles, I need to move," you protest. "I'm all filled with adrenaline."

He sighs. "Very well. I leave it up to you."

So, Slayer, do you train, or do you . . . do your nails?

SLAYER CH⊕ICE:

Do you decide to . . .

❨ train? *If yes, turn to page 236.*

❨ take a breather and do your nails? *If yes, turn to page 156.*

Okay, you decide to listen to your Watcher and not train.

You move to another part of the library because Giles thinks the ozone or whatever in fingernail polish is bad for his books. You have a few containers of polish and you line them up, admiring them.

"So, Purpleberry Plum or Shangri-la?" you ask Giles.

SLAYER ACTION:
Turn to page 152.

The deal is, you are really tired. No sleep, school all day, then training. You're going to have to try a little strategy.

Your shoulder rams against the library cage.

Aha!

SLAYER CHOICE:

Do you decide to . . .

❚ have a battle strategy based on what you did to Xander when he got possessed by hyena mojo? *If yes, turn to page 161.*

❚ try the Emily Dickinson approach? *If yes, turn to page 27.*

Spike looks intrigued. "Yeah? Let's have a go."
He opens his mouth and begins to sing:

SLAYER ACTION:
Turn to page 160.

"**W**hat?" Lyle frowns at you. "You can not!"

"Who's Emily Dickins?" Tector asks, halting his advance on you as you turn around to shake your head at him.

"Dickin*son*," you correct him disdainfully. With one eye on Tector, you say to Lyle, "Try it."

He pauses. "Um . . ." Then he sings: *"You left me two sweet legacies, A legacy of love."* He beams. "Hey! You're right!"

"And you're dust!" While he's being all happy, you dust him. Then you whirl back around and dust his stupid brother, who didn't even know Emily Dickinson's name!

SLAYER ACTION:
Turn to page 30.

"*Upon the gallows hung a wretch . . .*"

You're caught off guard. Emily Dickinson wrote *that*?

Spike takes advantage of your momentary distraction by throwing himself at you. You meet him straight on, ramming your fist into his face. His vampy mug snaps back, but he returns the punch, really hard!

You stagger, hit him. He staggers, hits you.

Stagger, hit.

Stagger, hit.

Blood.

Sweat.

Mucus.

You ram against the cage.

Against the cage.

The *cage.*

Remember the incident with the cage?

SLAYER ACTION:
Turn to page 161.

The cage!

You locked Xander in the library cage when he was possessed by hyena-ness!

You whip to the left, making a space between you and the entrance to the book cage. Spike steps right up to you, fists flying. He's laughing as he's hitting you, but hey, you're cornering him.

Drusilla says, "Let's all sing! About gallows and dying!" A glance out of the corner of your eye assures you that Giles is still holding her at bay.

"On all gallows' eve," Spike says as he punches you hard. "You fancy that, luv? Shall we string the Slayer up? By her intestines?"

"By 'er heartstrings," Dru says slyly. "She's in love. With Angelus."

Spike laughs. "She had any brains, she'd run like hell." He dodges your angry roundhouse kick. "Had a vampire yet, love? Once you've had dead, you can never go back. But we can change all that." He gives you a wink. "Fancy a toss, do you? I can see it in the way you glare at me."

"The evil eye," Dru says. "I'll give this one the evil eye. Make him do what I want!"

"Giles, you okay?" you yell.

"Good! You?"

"Good," you say back. Then you lunge at Spike, meaning to push him into the cage. But he dodges you, and you charge into the cage alone!

No matter. He gleefully charges in after you. You tuck yourself into a ball and execute a backward roll, knocking him off his feet as you exit the cage. As he's scrambling to his feet, you slam the cage door shut!

"Bloody hell!" he shouts, banging on the mesh.

With a satisfying *sniiiiiiick,* you insert the padlock through the hinges and snap that sucker shut!

At that moment, Drusilla rushes toward the cage, crying, "Spike?"

Giles races up to her and impales her with the wooden cross.

You whip a stake out of your trouser pocket and throw it at a stunned Spike, who gapes at the dust that was his crazy love. He's so overwhelmed, he doesn't seem to realize that he's been staked.

He explodes!

SLAYER ACTION:
Turn to page 163.

"**A**re you all right?" Giles asks.

You nod. "I should always listen to you," you say in a small voice.

"No matter." He adjusts his tie. "We accomplished the task. That's what counts." He smoothes back his hair. "Now, I want you to run along for a while. I need to do some serious research."

"Good. I'm gone," you say. You smile at him. "Witness me following orders."

"Yes, well, while you're running along, I do hope it involves some patrolling," he adds. "Some strange force is in action, and while I wish you could rest up from this fight, we must discover what is going on posthaste."

"Um." *Posthaste? Who talks like this?* "Patrolling." You nod. "Roger-dodger."

"Over and out." He points to the library's double doors.

SLAYER ACTION:
Turn to page 165.

It's easy! It's what a Slayer does! You fight fast and furious. Front kick, back kick. You're on fire!

Giles has Dru at bay with the cross from off the table.

"Slayer!" Spike says appreciatively. "What's gotten into you?"

"Boredom!" you cry. "I am bored with fighting you over and over! I will end you now!"

"Don't count on that," Giles calls helpfully.

"I will stake you twenty-five million times if I have to!" you bellow. You ram your fist into his face. His head snaps back, and the smile on his vampy visage just really pisses you off!

"Bloodthirsty thing, aren't you?" he drawls, wiping his own blood from his mouth as he advances on you.

"I am, Spike," Dru calls plaintively. "I'm very thirsty."

"Knickers on, pet," he says to her. "We'll have Slayer's blood for dinner tonight!"

"With cakes! And sausages!" she says.

"And librarian!" Spike adds.

"Not bloody likely," Giles retorts.

Then you hear the distinctive sound of a vampire turned to dust! *"Nooooooo!"* Spike shouts, turning his attention toward Giles and Dru—or where Dru was.

Score one for the Watcher, while the Slayer has yet to score. And . . . now you're even.

You grab a stake from your pocket and stake Spike!

SLAYER ACTION:
Turn to page 163.

You practically skip down the street, you are so happy to be out of the library and away from books about mucus, as well as actual globs of demonic mucus.

Ewww.

With the Pacific Standard Time and doing post-school slayery things, night's already falling.

There's a good band at the Bronze; you can hear the music at least a block and a half away as you move from the good part of town to the bad part of town. Which must be patrolled.

As you hurry to join the fun, you pass by kids you know from school—including a couple of Cordelia's Cordettes, who whisper about you as you pass. You try to ignore them, but you are acutely aware that popularity continues to elude you in Sunnydale.

You walk on; you can smell the delicious scent of espresso and the really, really big cinnamon rolls you sometimes share with Xander and Willow. You guys shared one at the fumigation party. . . .

Then you see him.

Owen Thurman. And he's with this other guy named Scott Hope.

It's still pretty weird with Owen, on account of your dumping him because he craved more wild nights slaying style, and you couldn't let him put himself at risk like that. Plus, secret.

Well, no matter. Angel's all boyfriendly with you now.

Plus . . . there *he* is.

It's almost like Angel already knew you were going to show. He's just out of the range of the street-lamp above the entrance to the Bronze, mysterious and broody in a most decidedly Bruce Wayne–like way.

He spots you, says nothing, but gazes at you as you walk up to him. You feel a little hesitant. Apparently, so does he. He just keeps looking at you without saying anything.

Then: "You want some coffee?"

"Yes," you tell him happily.

Then you two go in and sit at one of the high, round tables.

He says, "Espresso?"

"Mochaccino. You should try one too . . . except you can't taste anything. Right." You wince at your faux pas. He doesn't seem to mind, but then with Angel, it's hard to be sure. He doesn't smile all that much.

He disappears into the crowd. You look at the band, remembering how cool it was when Cibo Matto played.

And Angel is getting you coffee. As Willow says, it puts you in a relationship to have coffee.

You and Angel are having coffee!

You get a little happy thinking about that, but then you feel nauseated. Your stomach rolls, and you think, *It's happening again.*

And this time, it's happened enough times that your Slayer senses go on alert, and you start scanning for doubles. You see people dancing, people eating and drinking. Normal stuff. You see that young short guy, Jonathan, dancing alone on the dance floor. You can't ever imagine Jonathan doing anything to merit Slayer action, so you continue to gaze around the room.

Then you catch your breath. *No way. It can't be! Not again!*

Spike and Drusilla are standing on the catwalk above you. He's all normal face—well, normal for him—but Drusilla is vamped out. And she's got her arms around Scott Hope, who has no idea he's about to be chomped.

You push your way around some people on the dance floor. One of them is Amber, the cheerleader whose life you saved when she caught on fire, and she says, "Hey, hi!"

"Hey, hi," you reply, thinking, *Wow, a cheerleader said hi to me,* then refocusing on the unfolding Spike/Dru drama as you reach the stairs and clatter up them.

Spike notices you first. He grins at you and faces you head-on as if he hasn't seen you in a long time, saying, "Slayer! What a pleasant surprise! Well, actually not . . ." He jerks his head toward Dru, who is gazing at you over the shoulder of her intended victim. Scott clearly thinks they're making out. He's nuzzling her neck, which is ironic. 'Cuz she's not planning to "nuzzle" his.

"Hurry, pet," Spike says. "Slayer's here to spoil your fun."

"Let him go!" you shout.

Then you race at them—just as Dru throws back her head, then lowers it and sinks her teeth into Scott's neck like some happy drinking bird from hell. Or maybe a pig looking for truffles.

Both of these analogies are very, very gross.

Then, at that moment, Angel appears on the opposite end of the catwalk. He sizes up the sitch and says to you, "I'll take Dru!"

"Angel!" she cries delightedly, thrusting the wounded student away from her. Scott staggers and drapes over the side of the catwalk.

Dru sways toward Angel, singing, "The stars are singing! 'Run and catch, run and catch . . .'"

And you see that it is time for you to run and catch. 'Cuz Scott is about to fall off the catwalk.

Spike has vamped and is bouncing on the balls of his feet like a prizefighter. He puts himself between you and Scott and says to you, "Let's have a go, luv!"

"I got it!" Angel yells. "Get the kid!"

"Okay!" you shout, registering that Angel called a boy your age "a kid."

You ignore Spike and leap off the catwalk.

Dancers scatter as you land in a crouch. Then you

straighten into a standing position and hold out your arms just as Scott comes tumbling toward you.

You're aware that people are gonna wonder how you can manage to catch a tall, falling guy, but you'll have to figure how to explain that *after* you do it.

Also, in Sunnydale, people have a habit of explaining away things all by themselves . . . gangs on PCP? Broken gas lines? Please!

Then, out of the blue, someone yells, "I've got him!" and you are pushed out of the way.

It's Devon, the singer for Oz's band, Dingoes Ate My Baby. You're about to protest that no way will he get him—but Amber hurries up to you and cries, "Oh, my God, did you fall or what?"

Devon cries, "Whoa!" and gets out of the way.

Angel has joined the plummet! He's falling beside Scott!

Angel grabs Scott and manages to hit the floor first so the other guy lands on top of him. A stunned crowd surges forward, and you shift your attention to the catwalk. The tail of Spike's black coat is visible as the gruesome twosome melt into the astonished crowd.

Those two should be dead, you tell yourself. *Er. Dead-er.*

You know they're making a getaway, probably coming and going via the roof. You've used that way yourself before. You dash for the entrance to the

Bronze. There's so much confusion that no one notices as you race outside and into the alley, staring upward at the Bronze's roof as you go. There!

You see two figures moving beneath the moonlight. One is wearing a coat, and the other is gliding along beside him, waving her arms.

"Buffy," Angel says as he joins you.

"Wondering if there's a point," you say. "But if we don't, they might kill someone."

"Your call," Angel says.

Just then Cordelia comes flying out of the Bronze and accosts Angel. "Oh my God!" she cries. "Are you all right? That was so heroic!"

"Cordelia," you say, "we're kinda busy right now."

"Well, why don't you go take care of it yourself then, whatever it is," Cordelia says dismissively. Then she focuses all her grrrrlpower on Angel. "Can you drive me home? I'm all upset." She presses her fingertips to the bridge of her nose and begins to sniffle.

"Cordelia, we're kinda busy right now," Angel echoes.

"My car was just detailed," she adds, as if to tempt him. "It's a dream to drive. . . ."

While she's prattling on, you glance up at the roof again . . . and you don't see Spike and Dru!

"Angel," you say, gesturing, "I think we lost them."

He looks frustrated in his furrowed-forehead sort

of way. You both move away from Cordelia, who has some choice things to say about that.

Lucky for you, you're not listening.

"What do you want to do?" Angel asks you.

SLAYER CHOICE:

Do you decide to . . .

❚ go up on the roof? *If yes, turn to page 172.*

❚ search for them in the alley? *If yes, turn to page 182.*

You decide to go up on the roof. You know that there's an exterior ladder that runs up the back of the building. You say, "Ladder," and Angel's right there with you. You work so well together. That's one of the reasons you love him so much.

You go around the back and climb the metal rungs, *clang-clang-clang*. You're about to reach the top when Spike peers over the edge, raises his boot, and smashes it downward toward your hand!

SLAYER ACTION⊕:

If you didn't listen to your Watcher and pushed yourself too hard, turn to page 173.

If you listened to Giles and rested instead of overtrained, turn to page 180.

Ouch! Spike wears very heavy boots! You admit you let him take you by surprise. The only thing you can think to do is to reach for his ankle with your other hand.

He shakes you off like a dog shaking off water. The moonlight is shining straight down on him; all you can see is two hollows where his eyes should be, and his glistening fangs. He looks like a gargoyle as he sneers at you. "C'mon, then, fancy a dance?" he says. "You want to take me on?"

"No," you tell him. "I want to kill you."

"Fair enough. *I* want to kill *you*. We got unfinished business, you'n me." He grins and moves back, urging you to climb all the way up.

You manage to make it up the rest of the way and onto the roof. Dru is near the edge of the roof, twirling her fingers around.

"Oh, brought Captain Forehead as well, eh?" Spike says.

Angel is directly behind you. Then he fans right as you fan left, he going after Dru as you head for her sweetie-baby-cookie-honey serial killer boyfriend.

"Let's go. We ain't got all night," Spike says.

You're too tired to fight.

You pull out a stake and throw it hard. It flies through the air like an arrow shot from a bow . . . but it hits him in the left shoulder.

"Ow!" he shouts. "Wasn't countin' on any pain. Just a quick death for you and yours."

"Spike!" Dru cries, running from Angel. "I don't like it much! I want to leave."

You can see that Spike's worried about Drusilla, so you shout to Angel, "I'll head her off if she comes this way!"

"Leave her alone!" Spike yells. He rushes Angel, then feints a right. He doubles back, grabs Dru, and races for the edge of the roof.

They jump.

As they fall, Dru calls merrily, "We are flying!"

You and Angel race to the edge of the roof. You see that Spike and Dru have landed in the bed of a truck that appears to be filled with bags of trash. He gets to his feet and flashes you the British version of a nasty hand gesture, then collects Dru, who is still sprawled on her back.

The truck is moving, but you figure if you start running along the roof to keep up with it and time it just right, you can land in the bed.

"Buffy," Angel says, "not sure that will work."

He has a point. The truck is picking up speed and moving into a darker section of the alley. You're the Slayer, but you can still get seriously hurt. And you most certainly can die.

You exhale, making the tendrils of blond hair around your face waft like spiderwebs. You are ticked off that you let them flee.

What is with the bug analogies?

"Buffy . . . ," Angel begins.

"It's okay," you say sourly. "I'll get them another

time. And I'll kill them dead, just like Raid kills bugs."

He gestures at your face. "Your nose is running. Would you, ah, like a tissue?"

You touch the place between your upper lip and your nose (Giles probably knows the name for it). Gah! Mucus!

He says, "It's late. You're tired."

"Oh." You can't deny . . . he has a point there, too. "I promised Giles I'd patrol."

"Okay, then, let's go," he says.

You head for the ladder and look down below.

Angel comes up behind you and nuzzles you.

And then you see your mother!

At the Bronze?

If she's looking for you . . . you should get home as fast as you can! You should figure out another way down the roof and head for the hills! Or, at least, Revello Drive!

As you hesitate, Angel kisses the back of your neck. He nuzzles your cheek. Though his lips are cold, your skin warms. You begin to tingle. . . .

You turn your head . . . and think that you really shouldn't be doing this right now.

"Buffy," Angel whispers. He kisses you softly on your lips.

Do you kiss him back? Which you know from experience will start a chain reaction of heavy-duty kissage?

Remember, you have had several examples lately

that ought to convince you that when you blow off
what you should be doing, you pay. With your mother
searching for you, these smoochies might carry a high
price. Can you afford them?

SLAYER CHOICE:

Do you decide to . . .

\ stick around on the roof for some kissage? *If
yes, turn to page 178.*

\ go home as fast as you can? *If yes, turn to
page 177.*

"**A**ngel," you say reluctantly, "I have to get home. My mom's looking for me. Maybe Cordelia is still downstairs. She could give me a ride."

"You're right," he says, smiling at you with longing.

You peer over the side of the building. Your mom is nowhere to be seen. On a less busy night you might chance clambering down the opposite side of the building, where Spike and Dru jumped, but there are too many people around and there's already been too much excitement.

You climb down and go back into the alley.

SLAYER ACTION:
Turn to page 182.

Strappy little yellow sandals at Shoe Planet: $68
   That kick dress at Hot Topic: $109
   Smoochies with Angel: Priceless

And so you go for it . . . and go for it some more . . .
your eyes are closed and you are so loving this
moment, this perfect moment . . .

   . . . and you are still going for it . . .

   . . . when Angel says, "Suddenly I'm not feeling
very good." Then he gasps, *"Buffy!"*

   You open your eyes and . . .

   He explodes into dust!

   The dust that was your boyfriend scatters in the
night breeze.

   You begin to sob. You're numb. You're horrified.
You can't believe it. You simply can't believe it. You
lurch forward blindly, feeling for the dust, unable to
breathe. . . .

   And the thing that staked him is a little girl!

   She's dressed in clothes from long ago, and she
grins up at you and says, "Liam is my angel."

   Then she vamps. "My brother, my dear Angel
brother. I made him pay for what he did to us."

   "No." You shake your head. You don't know how
to make sense of this. You can't make sense of this.
Part of you understands that this must be a memory
creation from Angel's own mind. You know that he
killed his entire family, and he has been haunted by
guilt ever since he got his soul back.

   Past tense, Buffy. Angel is gone.

You can't accept that. You can't believe that.

Without warning, you attack the girl, yanking the stake away from her and plunging it into her heart. She dusts.

Now you are alone on the roof.

You made a very bad choice. A very selfish choice. As a result, Angel is gone.

You rise to your feet and stare up at the moon. Tears stream down your face. You vow that you will never, ever put your personal pleasure before your duty. You will stay alert. You are the Slayer. The lives of those you love depend on you.

You've learned your lesson. At a terrible price.

THE END

Not a problem, so much!

Because you're rested, you anticipate that Spike will try to smash your fingers with his boots. So you lift your hands off the rungs. Below you, Angel holds on to your calves to balance you. Then you leap up into the air and ram both fists into Spike's face as you clear the top of the ladder and hit the rooftop!

You are a mean, lean Slayer machine as you charge after Spike.

Angel shouts, "Right behind you!" and you both go into action. Spike looks shocked as he darts backward, shouting, "Dru! Poodle! Slayer's been eatin' her Weetabix! Best get out of here!"

"You've got that right!" you shout.

You slam your fist into Spike's face. He staggers back, touching his nose. Then he hits you back, right across the face. You execute an awesome roundhouse and connect with his kneecap. He yowls with pain.

Angel goes after Dru, who darts behind Spike. Angel races up beside you and hands you a stake, relay-race style. You bend your knees and hurtle through the air, preparing to ram into Spike, knock him down, then stake him.

Then Drusilla doubles over and cries, "Oh, I'm so ghastly ill!" Yes, she is mentally ill in a very ghastly way. But no problem. Soon she will be dust.

But suddenly there's another body in the middle of your trajectory. You slam into it and crash to the ground. Both you and it roll hard. You stop yourself to find that you're looking straight into the eyes of Darla, Angel's skank ho girlfriend, whom he dusted before your very eyes a year ago.

Darla blinks and says, "Who are you? Where are we?" She looks past you, and her eyes widen. "Angelus? What are we doing here? Aren't we in Prague?"

While she's distracted, you try to stake her. But she grabs your wrist and twists your forearm, trying to break it. You drop the stake. As you strain to free yourself from her grip, you pummel her in the stomach with your knee.

She slams her other fist into your face.

Angel races up, grabs the stake, bends down, and stakes Darla.

She explodes into dust underneath you.

You cast a glance at him to see if he's okay. He seems to be. He holds out a hand to you, and you jump to your feet.

You look around to discover that Drusilla and Spike are gone.

You say, "This keeps getting weirder. Let's go back to the Bronze and see if we can pick up some more clues."

SLAYER ACTION:
Turn to page 182.

You and Angel walk back toward the Bronze. You're ticked about losing Spike and Dru, but hey, walk with Angel, which is always wonderful.

The joint is jumpin', as they used to say (although you have no idea who "they" are). Willow and Xander are there! They wave at you. With both hands, like they're directing airplanes toward their hangers at the Sunnydale Airport.

They wave harder and mouth, *No! Go away!*

Ruh-roh, Slayer!

Beyond the semi mosh pit that is the dance floor of the Bronze, you see your mom! She's your stalker!

Is she with a *cop*?

"Oh my God," you murmur, tugging on Angel's sleeve. "I gotta book. Now."

But all he says is, "Buffy . . ." in that tone of voice you have come to recognize among your friends as the Sunnydale equivalent of "Houston, we have a problem." You think of it as the Monday Voice.

"What?" you ask as you look up at his face. He looks like he's seen a ghost. And could he get any paler? You never thought so before. And yet . . .

You furtively step behind him to shield yourself from your mother, and peer around to see what's giving your boyfriend a wiggins.

Okay, you see.

It's another Angel, staring back at the both of you!

"Okay, this is very weird," you say. "More than weird."

Remember the night you were going on a date

with Owen Thurman, and Angel showed up to warn you about the Anointed One, and he said, "You're on a *date*?" Remember how embarrassing that was?

This isn't like that at all.

IT'S DEEPLY SCARY.

Because it occurs to you that maybe the Angel who is standing beside you is *also* a double of Angel, and that is just creepy. Eyghon-creepy.

Then Angel Double walks up to you and says, "Buffy, I didn't bite your mother. You have to believe me," and he sounds exactly like . . . Angel! Then he glares at Real Angel—or at least you *hope* he's real. "Who the hell are you?"

Real Angel looks at him, then at you, and says, "Okay, this is more than weird."

You say, "Let's go outside and sort this out."

They don't look happy, but they do as you say.

You lead the two of them into the side alley and face them.

"Look," you say, "the real Angel knows exactly what's going on."

They both blink at you. "What do you mean, 'the real Angel'?" the one on the right says. "Of course I'm the real Angel. I'm here to find Darla. And stake her. Because she set me up, Buffy. She wants you to hunt me so that I'll have to kill you."

"Ha!" you cry. "You're the double! We've been through this. You staked Darla a year ago!"

"I . . . what?" Angel Double looks perplexed. "What are you talking about? The Bronze was empty just a second ago. Just you and me . . . and Darla."

Real Angel, who is standing on the left, takes a step away from the double and says, "Give me a stake, Buffy. I'm dusting this . . . thing right now."

You pull out a stake, but you don't give it to him. Instead, you say, "Angel, it would be too weird to watch you dust yourself. I would find it personally . . . not good."

"Dust?" Angel Double shouts. "Buffy, are you out of your mind? You are going to let that thing dust me? What's going on? That's some demon or something—I don't know—but it's obvious the Master sent him to confuse you. He's using a glamour to convince you he's me!"

And before Real Angel can stop him, Angel Double lunges forward and grabs the stake out of his hand.

"Give that back!" Real Angel yells.

Angel Double's response is to attack Real Angel. He leaps at him with the stake extended.

At that very moment, Spike and Drusilla leap down from above and land directly behind Real Angel. They faked you out.

"Bloody hell!" Spike cries as he straightens, then makes sure Drusilla is all right. For someone who is all weak and wafty, jumping from great heights doesn't faze her much. "What the devil's going on?"

"Spike!" Angel Double cries, shocked. "When did you get into town?"

"He is a mirror," Dru murmurs, swaying. "He casts a reflection, at last! Two of them, both for me!" She licks her lips and lets her eyelids droop in a sexy come-hither smile at both Angels. Which, on her, is pretty freaky, like Morticia Addams after too much Sambuco.

"Hey!" you protest, glaring at her. "Go get your own Angels!"

"This is gonna be fun," Spike says, cricking his neck left and right, as if to get the kinks out. He looks at the two Angels. "Either of you fancy playin' for our team?"

Angel Double glares at Spike and Drusilla. "Get out of town, now. I'll give you this one warning, because we used to run together."

"Like wolves," Drusilla giggles.

"We're not goin' anywhere, mate," Spike drawls. "This is our town now. We're gonna kill her and then take out the Anointed One."

Real Angel whispers to you, "I'm beginning to understand. These are like living memories. They're not real." He looks at you. "That's why they come back after we dust them."

"You're right." You swallow. "So you can, um, dust yourself if you want, I guess. Even though it will be deeply disturbing."

But as the two of you have been whispering, the others have started circling Real Angel.

A moment here, Buffy Anne Summers. Let the

action roll in slow-motion as you think about all those times—those many, many times—you were supposed to train with Giles and you did not. Instead, you:

1. were haben der big schmoochen in the cemetery with Real Angel.
2. went shopping for:
   a. shoes.
   b. other shoes.
   c. yet more shoes.
   d. sandals.

So this whole problem extends beyond training or not training earlier today. It's a fundamental problem with your approach to slaying.

Think about that as Drusilla, Spike, and Angel Double begin to circle your vampire-with-a-soul mate, with the express intention of turning him into ashtray fodder.

Resolve face, Slayer, and repeat after me: I will take my calling more seriously. This moment of clarity has been brought to you by the teeny little angel that sits on your right shoulder, i.e., your conscience. Oh, you may try to bargain with Fate for Angel's life: "I will train harder, I promise, if only you spare him. Please."

But here's the sitch, Miss Thing: You are the Chosen One. After Fate dealt you that card, it left the rest up to you.

So . . . are you slayer enough to save Angel? Have you learned enough moves, got strong enough muscles? Do you feel slayer-y today?

And . . . action!

SLAYER ACTION:
Turn to page 188.

And such action! You are Super-Slayer! You are a collectible action figure! Your vim and vigor kick in just like if you were a motorcycle and someone just kicked you into gear and then popped a wheelie!

Okay, that's just wrong. . . .

But hey, Buffy, who are you going to take out first?

SLAYER CHOICE:

Do you decide to . . .

❚ go for Spike? *If yes, turn to page 189.*

❚ go for Angel Double? *If yes, turn to page 191.*

You go for Spike, who is on the other side of the circle. You race toward him, jump into the air, and land on your left foot with your right leg extending and smashing right into his face. Then you drop both hands to the ground and kick up and back, with another direct hit!

Spike staggers backward, and Drusilla catches him. Which is impressive, given that she is about as substantial as a hologram of a toothpick. Have you noticed her arms? Yikes!

Then Drusilla vamps out, but you're not too worried about her. She's very weak from whatever her problem is.

And it dawns on you that you're the only real person in the batch. You've got three memory-thingies and a vampire boyfriend—who's being attacked by his double!

Yes, Angel Double is swiping at Real Angel with the stake. And quicker than you can say Mike Massa, the man who taught self-defense to the girls' PE classes, you join Angel in beating back the double! One-two, one-one-one-one with synchronized face pummeling, the new Olympic sport!

"Stop her, my Angel," Drusilla croons as Angel Double looks truly stunned at your attack on him and tries to duck you without hitting you back. "She is naughty and must have no cakes!"

"And no teeth, neither!" Spike shouts as he rushes back at you. He draws back his fist and aims it toward you like some big, forced perspective close-up in a cheesy movie with no budget, and it slams into your mouth.

You taste blood and, frankly, you don't know why vampires go all crazy over it.

"Why, Slayer!" he gloats. "What big lips you have! All the better to kiss you with, eh?"

The thought of kissing Spike is so disgusting that you lose your temper. You rage at him, swinging and kicking, really beating him back.

He just laughs as you split his lip. "What's wrong, then, touch a nerve? You want me, eh, Slayer?"

"I want you to end!" you shout, leaping into the air and double-kicking him in the face. Spike is so insane that he just laughs harder as blood runs from his nose and drips from his split lip.

Then Angel boots Angel Double in the chest, sending him slamming against the alley wall! Angel flies after him, pinning him against the wall. He hits him again and again.

A powerful blow from behind grabs your attention.

SLAYER ACTION:
Turn to page 191.

Spike hits you hard; you spin around, and then you ram your stake into Angel Double's chest! He looks at you the same way Darla looked at Angel—with wounded betrayal—and says, "Buffy?" right before he dusts.

SLAYER ACTI⊕N:
Turn to page 192.

And then the Angel beside you says, "Buffy, I still don't get where Darla is. I don't get this. I came here to kill her. Not . . . me." He touches his forehead. "Am I crazy? Am I really in an alley in New York? Whistler, are you here?"

"Oh my God!" Spike shouts, and bursts into laughter, pointing at you. "You dusted the wrong one!"

YOU JUST ACCIDENTALLY KILLED YOUR BOYFRIEND.

As you try to take that in, Drusilla says, "Watcher coming!" She links hands with Spike. "We'd better go!"

"Right, then," Spike says. He turns as if to leave, and then he wheels back around and stakes the remaining Angel.

That Angel dusts as well.

You break down sobbing.

Then behind you, Giles says, "Buffy! We must hurry!"

"Giles, Angel is dead! I killed him!" you wail.

"No, no, he's back at the school." He looks around furtively. Then he puts an arm around you. "Listen to me. Angel is alive. He brought us some information, and we need to get to work immediately."

You pull away. "How can I believe you? For all I know, you're a fake too! Oh, God!"

"Buffy, please, you must pull yourself together. Your mother is inside, looking for you. That young art intern confessed to her that you'd been by the gallery, and she's looking for you. And frankly, she's rather annoyed."

You let him lead you into the car. Willow and Xander are in the back. Willow puts her arms on your shoulders. "What's the matter, Buffy?"

Giles explains why you're so upset, and Willow gives you another squeeze from the back seat. "Buffy, Angel's okay. We're all okay. We're ourselves."

"Listen, we've things to tell you," Giles says as he starts up his clown car. "Angel did some checking around in the demonic underground. It seems that Ethan had teamed up with an ancient sorcerer named Lars Von Teufelsblut. He was quite the figure in the Middle Ages. It was said he had the ability to create doubles of individuals other persons kept in mind. People with whom they had unfinished business. Grudges—"

"Crushes," Xander chimes in.

"Apparently he has some strange demon who helps him. They delve into the mind of their victim and extract a memory, which then becomes reanimated. Or, in some cases, seems to take on a life of its own. It's tied to one's emanations."

You're listening. To his car engine. Which does not sound good.

"Lars Von Teufelsblut had a wife, Gisela. He simply adored her. According to Angel's sources, they were attempting some kind of interdimensional leap at precisely the wrong time." Giles pauses. "Guess when."

You sniffle. "Is Angel really okay?"

"Yes, Buffy," Willow assures you.

"Nineteen thirty-seven," he finishes. At your look, he nods. "When the Master was attempting to open the Hellmouth, they were trying to shift to another dimension."

"The mystical energies converged," Willow explains.

"Like the streams crossing in *Ghostbusters*," Xander adds.

"And Lars Von Teufelsblut was drawn here, to Sunnydale. He was imprisoned in a sort of suspended time warp."

"Guess where," Xander says.

"Are you sure he's really Angel?" you ask hesitantly.

"In the basement of the school," Giles reports. "However, Gisela was sent elsewhere. No one Angel talked with could say where.

"And it seems that Ethan came across Von Teufelsblut while he was looking for something else down in the basement, and they've struck a deal.

My guess is that Von Teufelsblut is helping Ethan acquire the Shimera demon and, in return, Ethan is attempting to free Gisela."

Sunnydale High looms on the horizon. Your heart thunders as Giles's little clown car putters closer to the school.

"I've also confirmed that it's the Shimera that's been eating people," Willow adds. "I hacked into the coroner's again tonight. There have been a lot more deaths than we realized. And the authorities have been studying the mucus, trying to figure out what it is."

Just then a cell phone chirrups. You're startled. You didn't know anyone had a cell phone.

"It's Miss Calendar," Willow announces. "We told her about what's going on. She's looking for information on the Internet. She gave me her phone in case she found anything." She pushes a button. "Hi, Miss Calendar? *What?*"

"What's wrong?" Giles asks, glancing at Willow in the rearview mirror.

"She's in trouble! The school is being attacked!"

"What?" Giles cries.

"What attacking?" Xander asks. "Who?"

"Everything. She says Von Teufelsblut is there, and he's got the weird creature with him. She recognized it. It's Der Luger. It's a demon, just like Angel said. It can read your mind and then make a double. Here!" She hands the phone to Giles.

"Jenny!" he says. "What's going on? Yes, yes, we'll be there shortly. Stay close to Angel. That's the safest place to be. Yes. Yes, I . . . I as well."

"Whaddup, G-man?" Xander asks.

"How many times must I ask you not to call me that," Giles mutters, very halfheartedly. You know he's worried about Miss Calendar. He's really fallen in love with her, and you're glad they've patched things up since she got possessed by Eyghon.

You find it within yourself to pat his hand. "Floor it," you tell him. "We'll get there faster."

"I am flooring it," he says between clenched teeth.

"When are you going to get a grown-up car?"

"This is a perfectly reasonable vehicle."

"Yeah, if we were running a theme park and needed kiddie rides," you mutter, but now is not the time to rag on him.

Because.

Oh.

My.

God.

Now is the time to stare in amazement.

Just as if someone has thrown a switch, the entire school lights up with shimmering blue energy. The windows flash and buzz as if someone is welding behind them all.

Giles pulls the car over, and everyone piles out.

Then, from across the street, Cordelia runs toward you. "Oh my God!" she shrieks. "I was coming back to get my cheerleading uniform out of my locker, and look!"

"How did you get here before us?" you ask, then shake your head. You know how. She has a real car.

"Have you . . . have you gone inside?" Giles asks, staring at the school.

"Are you crazy?" Cordelia asks.

"Jenny . . . ," Giles says.

"Hold on. Let me go in first," you say.

"No, we'll all go," Xander insists.

You turn and face them.

"Look," you say. "Here's the thing. I'm the Slayer. My head is filled with people and demons I can't seem to let go of. Sometimes I dream about people I couldn't save. Sometimes I dream about monsters I've killed. You've all seen some of my bad memories lately." You smile grimly. "But if you go in there, and we get animaniacal creatures from your minds, too, well, it's just that much more I'm gonna have to fight to save Miss Calendar."

"But we need to find out how to put a stop to it," Giles argues. "You won't be able to do this all by yourself."

"Giles is right," Xander says. "A mind is a terrible thing to waste."

"Okay, then." You're moved by their courage. "Let's go."

"Um, me too?" Cordelia asks anxiously. "Because . . . someone should guard the car."

"Oh, Cordelia, how kind," Giles says.

She blinks at him. "Not *your* car."

"Let's go, then," you say. "I suggest we fan out."

"You're the Slayer," Xander replies. "What you say, goes. How about I take the quad?"

"I'll take the library," Willow ventures.

"I'll go to the basement," Giles says. "That seems to be the apex of the activity.

"Also, where most of the stuff is going on," you say. "I'm going to patrol the school, look for Miss Calendar. Willow, I don't want you in there until we know what's going on."

You take a breath. "If any of you see Angel—"

"We'll tell him you're okay," Willow replies.

You all head toward the front of the school. You and Giles enter the school and jog down the main corridor.

The entire place is shimmering with blue. Immediately, you feel horrible. Giles doubles over and drops to his knees.

"Maybe you should sit this one out," you tell him as you help him over to the stairs. He sits on the bottom one with his head between his knees.

"No," he gasps. "I'll be all right."

"I don't think so," you say.

But you know he wants to find Miss Calendar. So do you. And Angel. That staking business has totally wigged you. You have to know that he's okay.

"Go on," he tells you. "I insist."

"Okay." You move off.

You walk down the corridor of Sunnydale High. Your school. The Hellmouth's school.

Shapes are brimming, forming. Then you see Miss Calendar's silhouette behind a pane of frosted glass on a classroom door.

You try the lock; when it doesn't work, you kick the door in!

All your Slayer senses are on alert, and they are crying, *Danger, Will Robinson.* And all those hours of training—

—er, ar, all the training you've shown up for . . . which has lately been not all that much, but hey, boyfriend, shopping, girl-time with Willow—

—comes to the fore as you crash open the door and find . . .

Ted! Your mom's robot boyfriend. In the flesh—or really good plastic, you never were clear on that.

Well, she said she dreamed about him. . . .

Wearing his I'm-so-normal, suburban-dad clothes, he's calmly perched on the corner of the teacher's desk, munching his world-famous, drug-infested chocolate chip cookies.

As you race down the center aisle between two rows of desks, he smiles at you and says, "Hi, little missy. Would you like some cookies?" He holds out a Baggie brimming with them.

"No, I'd like to bash your skull in!" you shout at him. "Except I already did!"

"Now, is that any way to talk?" he asks you, making a *tsk-tsk* face.

Then he stands up and tosses his cookies, so to speak.

As you launch yourself at him, you feel more dizziness.

The room is buzzing and swirling with blue. As vertigo overtakes you, Ted overtakes you as well! He slams his fist into your face, and you go staggering backward. You fall against a desk, the impact knocking the breath out of you.

He says again, "Now, is that any way to talk?"

The answer being no, since you can't talk right now!

Okay, Buffy, get it together.

SLAYER ACTION:

If you're tired from working out today,
turn to page 201.

If you only did the one training session with
quarterstaffs, turn to page 202.

For a moment all you see is stars. Then you pull yourself together and raise your head. For a second you think you're seeing double, because *two* figures are stealthily advancing toward you. But villain number two is not a clone of your mom's ex-boyfriend, Ted. It's Willow's demonic ex-boyfriend, Moloch!

Okay, the first time, I electrocuted him! you think. *In his own secret archvillain laboratory!*

And yet, here he is again, in all his weird cyber-ugliness, complete with curled demon horns and glowing LED eyes.

The dizziness recedes as the two grab your arms. You struggle as they haul you to your feet. Then Moloch makes a fist and hits you, hard. And it *hurts*!

Ted grabs you and starts shaking you. He's shouting, "Don't you want some cookies? I baked them myself."

He starts stuffing them in your mouth while Moloch hits you again.

You can't stop them!

Then you hear chanting.

You look up.

SLAYER ACTION:
Turn to page 203.

Y ou feel a wave of dizziness, but no way do you let Ted get anywhere near you. As he tries to sock you, you duck, managing a truly awesome roundhouse slam into his solar plexus. He goes "ooph" just like a real person, but you aren't fooled.

You spiral down as you place your hands on the floor and kick at him with both your feet. Once you know you've made impact, you do a front flip and turn in the air, landing facing him.

And he's with Moloch, the robot-demon who had the hots for Willow!

I electrocuted that sucker!

But you don't give any more thought to thinking; it's distracting, and you need your well-honed fighting skills right now. The two bad guys start pushing desks out of the way like flimsy pieces of balsa wood—*what does a balsa tree look like, anyway?*—as they come for you.

Except for the element of surprise, they've got nothing on you.

You pick up a desk and whirl in a circle. Ted goes flying across the room.

Then you throw the desk at Moloch. He staggers backward. You look around for a handy live electric wire—also some water—but there is none to be had.

Then you hear chanting.

You turn to the doorway.

SLAYER ACTION:
Turn to page 203.

It's Miss Calendar. And she has a laptop!

"By the power of the circle of Kayless, I command you, demon, come!"

Moloch starts waving his arms and bellowing in his weird demon way. Then he explodes!

She drops her laptop as it bursts into flame!

"Thanks," you call to her as you glance over your shoulder.

Then she shouts, "Buffy!" and points to your left.

Ted is on the move again. He's shouting at you, "Don't you want to buy some software? It's the best software ever made. It's error-free. It's error-free." His face starts twitching. You have the strangest feeling of déjà vu.

So . . . you go to work.

And Ted flies apart! His head goes soaring into the air. He says, "Let's play mini-golf! Let's make pizza!"

His headless body staggers around until you give it a few more pummels.

Then it falls over. Electricity buzzes all over it.

"Thanks," you say to her. "You're okay. Angel?"

"Fighting," she tells you. "Last I saw him, he was holding his own."

"How did you find me?" you ask her.

She smiles. "Giles. He was on his way to the basement."

"Check," you say. And then . . .

SLAYER ACTION:
Turn to page 204.

You finish staggering from the dizziness as you approach Giles down in the basement. Blue light flickers everywhere. There's a buzzing in your ears. But maybe that's normal.

He's bending over a red circle inscribed with a pentagram and a statue of a Greek guy with two faces. The silver canister you saw Ethan steal from the art gallery lies on its side at Giles's knee. It has been sheered open.

The entire place is crackling with energy. "Buffy! You're all right," Giles says.

"No." You swallow hard. You are so wigged. "I'm a double."

He gapes at you. "But how . . . ?"

"Because it doesn't make sense for me to be here already. I was just with Miss Calendar. And now I'm here. With no walk in between." You tremble. "I think since I . . . she was already aware of the doubling magicks, I've carried that awareness into . . . double-hood. So I know I'm a fake."

He looks equally shaken. "You must be wrong."

You shrug. "And yet." You point at the statue. "What's going on?"

He gets back on track. You've always admired that about him, his ability to focus.

Or . . . Buffy has always admired that. If you think about this too much, you'll wig.

"Well, I spoke briefly to Jenny. It seems Ethan is up to his old tricks. Fomenting chaos, as it were.

Specifically to keep you . . . er, to keep the Slayer preoccupied while he works behind the scenes."

You're not surprised in the least. "Because . . ."

"There have been stories of a treasure deep in the basement of this school. And there is, of a sort. It's the Shimera demon itself. It is exquisite, covered in gems and gold, as I said. Perhaps he tempted Von Teufelsblut with it. It was trapped during the earthquake of nineteen thirty-seven, much as the Master was. Ethan found a way to release it."

You take that in. "Because . . ."

He exhales as he picks up the head and stares at the hideously contorted frown on one of the faces. "Because it is capable of devouring dimensional space. It can literally eat its way through the portals of our world."

"Oh, great." You sigh. "And Ethan is hot to do this why?"

"Well, it seems that on the Feast of Janus, the Shimera demon can devour enough of our dimensional space to allow Janus to enter our world."

"The God of Chaos," you say.

"The god that Ethan worships above all others." Giles taps the silver canister, showing you the engraving on the side. It reads SHS 1937.

"It appears that this time capsule held this particular statue. Which is, of course, cursed."

"Of course," you say tiredly. "But who buried it?"

"That remains a mystery that perhaps one day

we'll solve. But I think it's safe to say that Sunnydale is rife with people who worship the dark gods."

"Probably the school principal back in nineteen thirty-seven," you grouse.

"He must be stopped at all costs. This very night."

"Because tonight is the Feast of Janus," you conclude. It doesn't take a rocket scientist. It's always tonight. Or on the next full moon. Especially if it's on a Monday.

"Indeed." He adjusts his glasses. "It all falls together on this unholy night of nightmares." Giles looks around. "The blue energy field is emanating from Der Luger, the demon Von Teufelsblut has with him. I have been striving to keep my mind clear of thoughts of anyone. But I've spoken of Jenny, and I . . . I was wondering how you are."

As he speaks, Jenny Calendar appears, as if from thin air. She looks around and says, "Rupert? How did I get down here?"

Giles looks at you, and you at him. You say softly. "I have to go."

"Buffy . . . ," he says.

You meet his gaze. "If you get in trouble," you tell him, "keep me in mind."

"Buffy, what are you doing? What am I doing here? I feel awful," Jenny says. "And . . . so sad."

"I believe that's an effect of the Shimera," Giles says.

You say to Giles, "I'll go check on Willow and Xander. Then . . ."

"Then . . . be careful," he replies.

"I will," you promise. But you know something he's too polite to say: As a double, you're expendable.

SLAYER CHOICE:

Do you decide to . . .

\see how "you" and Xander are doing? *If yes, turn to page 208.*

\see how "you" and Willow are doing? *If yes, turn to page 210.*

"**X**ander!" you shout as you wake into existence beside the Slayer's friend.

He flashes you a big smile. "Wow, hey! Am I glad to see you!"

And no wonder. He has been driven into the auditorium . . . by a throng of vampires headed by Absalom, the Master, and Xander's old friend Jesse. You and he stand at the top of the bleachers, and the monsters are charging up them!

Xander is armed with a cross and a stake, but you know from personal experience that the Master can eat stakes for breakfast—or, at least, hold on to them—if he wants to. It's a whole big ego thing, probably a way to pick up vampire chicks.

"And here I am," you say. The army of monsters is only three steps away! You can smell their fetid breath. The roar is deafening.

"We have to get you out of here!" You turn to him. "Xander, listen to me! I'm not Buffy! I'm a double. Think of me! Think of me a lot! Keep me in mind, and don't stop thinking of me!"

His cheeks redden. "Since we're gonna die, I guess I can tell you I hardly ever do stop thinking of you!"

As he speaks, a copy of you pops into existence. And another! And another!

"What the heck?" he says, and then he realizes.

Soon, there are a dozen of "you," maybe two, and you move into Slayer mode! And the weird thing is, some of you fight better than others, and some of you die more quickly than others.

And a lot of you die very brutally: heads cut off; throats torn open; Slayers beaten to death.

Slayers torn limb from limb by Luke and the Master; stomped in the face by Spike; eyes poked out by Drusilla, who then slashes your throat.

But all of you fight to the death, protecting Xander as he makes his way out of the gym. He may not be the best fighter, or the strongest, but his huge heart and his courage fill you with admiration . . . and gratitude that he is your friend.

Buffy's friend . . .

And then you're suddenly in the quad, and you realize that the Buffy "you" were must have been killed, and you are a new one.

And if the gym was a nightmare, then the quad is what the dreams of the damned are like. . . .

SLAYER CHOICE:

Do you decide to . . .

\ go to Willow? *If yes, turn to page 210.*

\ go to Angel? *If yes, turn to page 213.*

\ remain in the quad? *If yes, turn to page 215.*

"**W**ill!" you cry as you race toward her.

She's in the basement with Miss Calendar and Giles, as you are now too. It's the Sunnydale High basement of today, bathed in a sea of blue energy . . . and there are about a dozen people milling around, dressed like extras in a Dracula movie!

The men are wearing blousy white shirts, embroidered vests, and baggy pants. The women have on colorful skirts, white blouses, headscarves, and lots of gold jewelry. You realize they're Gypsies. You turn to Willow and say, "Who are these people?"

She stares at you. "So it's true. You . . . you're . . . a double. We . . . we've been though this already. They're Gypsies. They just showed up. Popped into the basement, around the time Miss Calendar showed up, um, this last time that she showed up."

You gaze around. "Why Gypsies?"

"We don't know!" Miss Calendar says. She seems very agitated. Well, duh. Who isn't?

And then . . . a terrible despair overcomes you as the room falls into darkness. You gasp, and fall to your knees. You are awash in fear.

Willow finds your hand. "We were expecting this," Willow shouts in your ear. "Remember? We've called the Shimera demon. . . ."

"No, I don't remember. The last thing I remember is fighting Moloch," you tell her.

"Then you're from me," she tells you, squeezing your hand. "You're part of my memory. Because I was wishing you were here. Because I'm, well, I'm really scared, Buffy." Her eyes are wide, her face pale.

"I'll protect you," you promise. You look at all of them. "I'll protect you all, or . . . die trying."

The room falls completely silent, though you can tell that there still are a lot of . . . Gypsies . . . in the basement. You feel the heat of their bodies. You smell scented oils.

You hear weeping.

"Apparently, this is how the Shimera overcomes its victims," Giles whispers in your other ear. "One is overwhelmed, rather like a mouse facing down a cobra."

"I felt that way at the art gallery, but there was no demon snake there," you argue.

"Perhaps it was underneath you. Ethan may have been procuring a sacrifice for it . . . and I would venture to guess that Von Teufelsblut and Der Luger were also present, using their magicks to create a double of you."

He clears his throat and adds, "This is another double of Miss Calendar. Only this one doesn't seem to realize it. So she is from another part of my memory. The Gypsies are very upsetting to her."

What's up with that?

And then the voice of Ethan Rayne rings out over the hushed, frightened crowd.

"Rupert!" he shouts. "What the deuce are you doing down here?"

You look around, but you don't see him.

"Show yourself, you bloody maniac," Giles yells. "We're going to defeat you, so you may as well give it up now."

Ethan's answering laugh really pisses you off.

SLAYER CHOICE:

Do you decide to . . .

\ go to Angel? *If yes, turn to page 213.*

\ go to the quad? *If yes, turn to page 215.*

Angel stands with his arms around you.

His dark eyes are staring at you. You feel the strength in his arms, the sanctuary of his presence.

Shouting and screaming surrounds you, but your voice is a hushed whisper as you say, "My blood is . . . off."

"So you know," he whispers back.

You are sheltered beneath a tree in the quad, but they are coming. The monsters are everywhere. The carnage as they attack the humans of your memory— of Buffy's memory—is hideous.

They have not found you and Angel yet.

But they will.

You sense that this moment is one given to you to say good-bye.

"I know that I'm not real," you tell him. "And yet . . ."

He tightens his embrace. Blue lightning flashes around you. Jags of energy shoot into the grass, setting it alight. Tall flames join the swirling blue. You feel horribly ill. As if you were dying.

"And yet . . . ," Angel says.

You kiss. Deeply. Passionately.

We could do other things, you think wildly, knowing that seconds exist between this moment and the rest of eternity. *I could have that with him.*

You move your head back and whisper, "If I'm not real, it doesn't matter what we do . . . if you remember me . . . if you survive, we can . . . do whatever we want."

"I wish," he says. "But it doesn't work that way, Buffy. It's not who does it, it's what is done."

Then someone shouts, "Over here! The Slayer! Get her!"

"Remember me," you beg. "If you survive."

He shakes his head. "We'll both survive. Because neither of us is here."

Of course. He's a double too.

And then they're on you. . . .

Angel puts his arms tightly around you, and you kiss as if there's no tomorrow. . . .

SLAYER ACTION:
Turn to page 215.

*O*h, *this is so weird,* you think as you race into the quad. *Talk about a wiggins.*

All through the history of Sunnydale High, there have been stories about it being haunted. Some people have seen the ghosts of teachers; others, of students. You wouldn't be a bit surprised if the entire place needed to be exorcised.

Like, right now.

Awash in crackling blue light and huge zigzags of strobelike lightning, and a shrieking and screaming like an army of banshees, the entire quad of Sunnydale High School is packed with every demon you've ever fought. There's the Master. And Luke. And another Master.

There are so many of you that you can't count them.

You are feeling very sick, so you imagine they're emanating from you . . . or from the mind of the Slayer, if she's not you.

If you think about this too much, your head is gonna hurt.

On the second-story balcony that overlooks the quad, an extremely ugly creature leers. Maybe at one point it was a person, but it is even less human-looking than the Master. It has black holes for eyes, and purplish-green skin pulled over a skull. Horns protrude from its head and curl into ultra-sharp points. It's wearing a black robe spangled with stars and moons.

Beside it, perched on the balcony railing, is a bizarre, gargoyle-like frog thing. The blue light is emanating from its belly. Its bulging eyes grow bulgier, until it looks like one of those Martian Popping Things that Xander's friend Jesse had in his locker—

And as you think that, Jesse pops into existence, directly in front of you!

"Hey! Where's Xander?" Jesse asks. Where am I? You're that new girl, Buffy, right?" Evidently he has come into existence from a time before he was turned into a vampire.

The horned being in the robe stretches forth his hand and says something in sorcerer-speak to Jesse. Then Jesse's eyes glaze over, and he takes a step forward.

Your mind fleetingly touches on other humans you've lost to the dark side of the force.

And Billy Ford pops into existence.

"Stop that!" you shout. And then that weird friend of Billy's named Diego appears. And that blond Goth chick. Some of the kids who were massacred during the Harvest show up next, their faces at first alert and terrified, then slackening as Von Teufelsblut works his evil mojo on them. Next come several of the victims of the devouring beast that started you out on this adventure in the first place—in the flesh, with all their bones.

They are all appearing in the space between you

and the bad guys, a silent army, waiting to do Von Teufelsblut's bidding.

And speaking of bad guys . . .

They also pop into existence, but all of them are grouped behind the humans who have been brought forth. Here's Moloch *again.* And Ted. And the Master. And Luke. There's at least a cast of fifty, and they're multiplying. It's like Der Luger has an unlimited budget to re-animate or re-create every single villain who has ever plagued you to star in your life. Talk about your psycho Looney Tunes!

"Okay, listen, I have no quarrel with any of you," you tell them all, both the good and the evil, the dead and the deader. "At least, not now. So step aside, and nobody gets hurt."

Von Teufelsblut shouts some words in Latin— you guess, or maybe French—and all the human memory constructs take two giant steps forward, placing themselves squarely in the front line against you—acting as human shields between you and all the monsters.

This isn't fair.

You are the Slayer, and you have no right to harm human beings. Obviously, Von Teufelsblut knows that. It's practically part of your DNA. But these aren't really human beings. However, it takes your breath away to see how many people you remember—people whom you couldn't save. Old ladies, little kids . . . Jesse. The sheer number stuns you. And even more upsetting is that you remember each one very clearly—you recall seeing the looks on their faces as you had to watch them die because you couldn't get there in time. The sheer terror, the pleading—*Do something, quick!* The crazed rictus of the vamp faces of those who had been turned—Jesse and Ford, for two. But there have been others, so many others.

Each one has never left your mind. Is it any wonder that there are some nights you can't sleep?

They shuffle toward you, the monster-memories bunched up behind them. You see the strategy. Any moment now, they're going to attack you, and you'll have to plow through the human memory constructs to get at them.

And then . . .

. . . you are on the balcony directly in front of the nightmarish figure and the gargoyle. Just you, and them . . . and you have no memory of arriving here. So you know the bad news.

You're a double!

"You will not stop Ethan Rayne from rescuing Gisela," Lars Von Teufelsblut shouts from the balcony.

"Newsflash, Skeletor!" you fling back at him. "He's *not* going to rescue your girlfriend. He never was! He only promised you that so you would distract me. He doesn't care about you. He's trying to capture the Shimera demon and let Janus into this dimension!"

His eyes bulge almost as big as the gargoyle's—Der Luger?—as he cries, "Liar!" He raises his arms, and the spangles on his robe glitter in the weird blue light.

You've clearly touched a nerve. It's dawning on him that Ethan might be double-crossing him. You'd think hanging out with someone named The Liar would make you more cautious about people lying to you.

Von Teufelsblut shouts more, and all the doubles head for you.

"I don't want to hurt you," you call to the humans. "But you're not real. So I can hurt you, if I have to. And I will." *God, I'm so glad my friends aren't here. . . .*

"What are you talking about?" asks a familiar voice as Xander appears. And Willow appears beside him!

"Will? Xand?" you ask. "No, I don't want to fight you, please. Go away!"

"You're that new girl. Cordelia's friend, Buffy," Willow says wistfully. "You shouldn't hang out with us. It'll mess up your social life."

"Go away," you beg them. "Get out of here."

Then Von Teufelsblut moves his hand, and the two take on the same glazed look as the others.

"Please! Go!" you desperately try again. "This isn't your battle. It's mine."

Beside Von Teufelsblut, Der Luger whirls and glows

with blue energy. You feel drained, like Superman around Kryptonite. You swallow down bile as sweat breaks out on your forehead.

Think of no one else, you order yourself.

But of course she appears: your mother, Joyce Summers, who for one moment registers recognition, then stares straight ahead, zombie-like. Then Giles winks into existence beside her, saying, "There's a reason why you're here, and a reason why it's now," and then goes blank as Von Teufelsblut waves his hand.

Miss Calendar appears next.

Then George Handley.

Oz.

Dr. Koneff.

Principal Flutie.

Principal Snyder.

And more of the bad, or the badly misguided: Ampata and Miss French. Darla and the Anointed One. There are the Gorch brothers. And Marcie Ross, very visible. And that vampire who went after Owen Thur—

Whoops.

Owen Thurman appears.

I need to stop thinking, stop remembering.

You stare at the figures ranged in front of you.

You fill your mind only with the impending battle.

I am Buffy the Vampire Slayer, or I am here in memory of her.

I am here to fight, and I will keep fighting until I die.

No matter how many times it takes.

"Slayer! I challenge thee!" Von Teufelsblut's heavily accented voice rings out in the crackling blue. Der Luger's eyes bulge, and the creature shudders and shakes. You're standing in a crackling energy field, and you feel terribly ill. Bile rises in your throat; all you want to do is fall to your knees and retch.

But you stand tall as your gaze sweeps from the ancient sorcerer and his minion to the figures he has pulled from your mind . . . and your heart. They are an army of everyone living inside your head—your fears, your dreams, your hopes, your failures.

Those you love.

Don't think about him. *The one you love. Don't.*

You resolutely lift your chin.

I am Buffy the Vampire Slayer. I am the one girl in all my generation chosen to fight the vampires and demons—and all the other dark forces that prey on humanity. I am their only hope.

I am their Champion.

And no matter how many times I fall during this battle . . . I will rise up again, and I will save the world.

Von Teufelsblut smiles evilly at you. You do not smile back. The figures between you shift; you feel the tension rising. Adrenaline floods your body.

"Do you accept my challenge, warrior maid?" Von Teufelsblut prods you.

"I have no choice," you reply, head raised high.

"Of course you do." He holds out a hand, or what

passes for one. Bones and talons; could he really have been a person once? "You can join our side. Once Gisela is free, we will usher in a new world." He talks like a Nazi in a bad black-and-white forties movie.

"Sorry," you say. "Not big on ushering. You never get to see the movie all the way through, and have *you* ever swept up that much buttered popcorn?"

"Your humor is as feeble as you are," he retorts, filled with contempt.

"Then meet this feeble," you shoot back. *"Now."*

"You are challenging *me*?" His smile grows. "Delightful! I accept!"

This is it. The final showdown.

"Avaunt!" he shouts to his army.

And they charge, waves of memory-beings racing at you. You prepare to defend yourself.

To defend the human race.

The first one to reach you is your mother. You take a breath, say, "I'm sorry, Mom," and kick her in the solar plexus.

She feels like a real person as she grunts and falls.

Then Willow races at you from the left, and Xander from the right. You rise into the air and kick out your legs in a split, smacking both of them in their jaws.

Willow staggers backward, but Xander comes at you again.

Then it's Cordelia who moves forward.

Then George Handley.

You mow through the people-memories.

And the monsters come at you from between the

bodies. The Master reaches you as Luke holds you for him; you smell his breath as he leans in for the kill. . . . He bites hard.

It hurts.

You pop back into existence as Spike sinks his teeth into you.

You reappear as Giles Double raises an ax above his head and Angel Double pins you to the ground. Willow, Xander, and your mother watch as the ax arcs down toward your neck.

There's a searing pain—

You retch under a tree in the quad, violently sick and very dizzy, as you . . . realize you can't beat him. He kills you every time. You are despairing.

That means the Shimera demon is nearby.

You have no idea what to do. You sweep your gaze over the balcony and see your friends . . . or doubles of your friends . . . dying in awful ways. You force yourself to turn away because, once again, it is *not real.*

You see Angel dusted by Darla. Drusilla walks across the grass, dancing with Jesse's head dangling from her fingertips.

We can't win.

I can't win.

Your despair is overwhelming. You are sobbing, and so sick to your stomach, you can barely move.

Then there's a terrible rumbling as the ground begins to shake. The buildings all around you start to crumble.

It's a major earthquake!

Pieces of masonry fall. You look up and—

SLAYER ACTION:
Turn to page 225.

You are straddling the Shimera demon, speaking a strange language Giles has taught you. Your bleeding legs cling to its sides, and you taste the strange brew Giles gave you to drink, to combat the despair the demon casts into its victims to immobilize them.

The demon is soaring into the air, and the thick blue field around you is boiling and steaming. You are in incredible pain, but you hang on as the demon races into the sky.

You think of everyone who is counting on you, and you see doubles of them down below you, still fighting, still dying.

The Shimera is long, with an elongated head like a Chinese dragon, and a fluted, webbed back and huge, leathery wings. It is covered with shining jewels, and it is emitting flame into the blue as it flies.

You are hanging on, and you know you're a double. But you're a double of Buffy the Vampire Slayer.

And you cannot let the Shimera devour her dimension. It is very close to achieving Ethan's final aim, and you are the only one who can stop it.

The demon opens its mouth wide and waggles its head from side to side, giving you a view of its huge fangs, glistening and gleaming. As it clacks its jaws, thunderous sounds like sonic booms shake the buildings and grounds of the high school below. Mucus—of course!—ropes from its two enormous incisors. Then it roars and shoots flame into the night sky.

A piece of sky is actually *missing*: There is only gray space, a neutral, empty vacuum.

The Shimera demon roars and sinks its teeth into the sky beside the horrifying void.

You have weapons to fight this. You have come armed. You know that in the basement, Giles, Miss Calendar, and Willow are invoking spells to aid you.

From the vacuum, a huge eye glares at you. Its center is completely black, but shapes move and spin inside it. You see the Old Ones inside that eye, capering and cheering in hell dimensions within hell dimensions within hell dimensions, waiting to pour into your world.

The eye of Janus!

And then you lift up your hands and shout the ancient words Giles taught you:

"Shi watanga, mea filtata—"

It is a sorcerer's language; it is a spell designed to hurt a god.

Then the entire sky bursts into flame. Fireballs erupt, and you fly right into one.

It hurts. . . .

SLAYER ACTION:
Turn to page 227.

"**N**ein!" Lars Von Teufelsblut screeches as Angel holds him back.

You and the vampire have finally reached the balcony. You don't know how many times you had to battle to reach it, but you are finally here.

Giles, Miss Calendar, and Willow have magickally aided you, and this is the moment you have fought so hard for.

Von Teufelsblut struggles in Angel's grasp. Both of them are covered in blood, and there is a deep gash across Von Teufelsblut's neck. Did Angel bite him? You can't remember.

You are holding on to Der Luger, and its bulging eyes are wild with terror. Its skin feels very froglike. The air around you is so blue, you can hardly see. You are shaking with illness, and the awful despair emanating from Der Luger is almost more than you can handle, despite all the help you're getting.

I've lost so many . . . if I survive, I'll lose so many more. . . . I don't deserve to be the Slayer. I should just give up, and let someone more worthy have my place. . . .

"Buffy, do it!" Angel shouts at you.

No. I am Buffy the Vampire Slayer.

I am the only one who can stop this!

With a grunt, you slam your fists into the belly of Der Luger. You touch a strange, hot mass—its energy center, just as Giles told you. It is pulsing with energy; Giles conjured up a numbing potion so that you could do this, but the pain is hideous. Sweat runs down your face as your flesh burns.

Gritting your teeth, you grip your hands around the searing object and steady yourself, preparing to yank the energy center out. That will end everything . . . for you.

You will cease to exist.

And just before you do it, you have a moment's hesitation.

The survival instincts of a slayer are very powerful. . . .

And as you hold the beating core of Der Luger's memory-creating power, you relive the strongest memory Der Luger has absorbed. It is the singular vision that has kept Lars Von Teufelsblut bent on his course all these years—the memory of his one true love:

She is Gisela, and she is so very beautiful, with her long, blond braids and her enormous blue eyes. Her lips, rosy and soft. Her skin is like fresh milk. And as hideous as Lars Von Teufelsblut has become—from worshipping his dark gods for so many centuries—she loves him.

The Knights Templar have discovered them, and are coming for them in their castle, Schloss Von Teufelsblut—Castle of the Blood of the Demon. They will torture them, and then they will burn them alive.

"It will not happen," he promises her. *"I will transport us to a safe place."* He snaps his fingers, and Der Luger bounds over to them.

Energy crackles around them. It is fierce, and terrifying, as blue surrounds them.

They rise into the air as the Knights burst into the room.

They travel through space, and time, in a golden sphere . . .

. . . until something goes wrong.

A vortex of foreign energy envelops them! It is ochre, as vile as rotten flesh and there is a face swirling in it. It is a king vampire, and he shouts, "No! Get out of here!"

Everything explodes.

Gisela screams as something drags them down, deep down, and buries them in mud and rock and something gelatinous, that stinks of the grave.

And when Lars Von Teufelsblut wakes, Der Luger lies unconscious beside him. But Gisela is gone.

All this you see as you prepare to kill Der Luger.

You gaze at Lars Von Teufelsblut, who is hideous beyond the telling, and announce, "Say good-bye to her and everything else. Forever!"

He hits you with magicks, green and silver jags of energy shooting from his hands. He is surrounded by glazing, white-hot beams that rip directly into your body. You can feel yourself shredding apart.

You die in agony.

. . . and he attacks you with magicks, lightning-sizzles of emerald and platinum that slice into your flesh and rip it apart. The pain is unbelievable . . . as you die.

. . . Lars Von Teufelsblut, the most feared sorcerer of the Dark Ages of humankind, assaults you with his most potent magicks as you fight to save the world.

Your last defense is the spell Giles taught you:

"Shi watanga, mea filtata—"

Your resulting death is so awful that you remember it the next time you pop into awareness.

. . . and you squeeze Der Luger's source of power, the throbbing, viscous energy mass, squeeze until your forehead breaks out in blood as you feel yourself jittering apart.

There is a terrible, deafening roar. All around you, the world shatters; for a strange, long moment you see reflections of yourself, stretching in all directions. You see your contorted expression; you see agony in your eyes; you are weeping and pleading. You are begging not to be hurt. Not to feel this unbelievable pain. It is excruciating. It is unbearable.

It does not go away.

If I have to endure it, don't let me remember it, you silently beg. Tears of blood slide down your cheeks as your eyes sizzle away; as your lips curl and crack. As you suffer as no living creature should ever suffer.

Don't let me remember a moment of it.

Don't let me remember—

SLAYER ACTION:
Turn to page 232.

It is over.

Exhausted, burned, and battered, you are still standing.

Giles and Angel, Willow, Xander, and Miss Calendar flank you as doubles of monsters and nightmare memories wink out of existence. The fiery sky becomes shadowy midnight. Clouds roll gently across the moon.

There is a moment of silence. It is too grave a victory for cheering.

"We did it," you say.

"Yes," Giles replies. Miss Calendar is standing beside him, her face pale and bruised.

You look up uncertainly at Angel, who has his arm around you. He has been gravely wounded—there is blood on his chest and his face—and the expression on his face speaks of his relief that you're beside him.

"Am . . . I?" you ask.

"You're you," he assures you. "You're Buffy."

He takes your hand. With Xander and Willow behind you, holding each other carefully, you and the others walk from the school toward the street.

Cordelia runs toward you.

"Oh, thank God!" she cries.

You're touched by her concern.

"My car is untouched! Can you believe it?"

You say, "That's just so fabulous."

And the funny thing is, it's true.

"So what happened?" she asks. "I was going to come join you all, but, well, there was so much screaming!

And blueness. And this dragon was flying up and eating the sky!"

Angel smiles at her.

"You did come," he says. "You just don't remember it."

"You fought really well, too," Xander adds.

She looks stricken. "And now?"

"Now, you're guarding your car," you say. "Into which I will sit, and you will drive me home so I can lie to my mom about where I've been."

"But I don't remember what happened!" Cordelia protests.

"We chanted down in the basement, and the Shimera died, thus preventing it from devouring dimensional space," Giles explains. "Janus could not come through. Ethan ran off somewhere. Buffy—or one of her, ah, associates, rather—killed Der Luger and Der Teufelsblut. Once Der Luger was destroyed, all the memory doubles ceased to exist."

"Oh." She shrugs. "Okay."

You walk around to the passenger side of the car. Angel goes with you.

You gaze up at him.

"Later tonight?" he asks. "Cemetery?"

"On my list," you reply. But it is a list. You have grave responsibilities. You accept that now. You have learned your lesson . . . if there was a lesson to learn in all this.

You are the Slayer. You must always remember that.

You turn to go. Then you look at him very seriously

and say, "Angel . . . I want happy memories."

He looks at you with such emotion. Such longing. You feel so alive. So . . . real. The one girl in all the world . . . who is loved by Angel.

The Slayer, on a quest she must undertake alone . . . unless someone is willing to walk in the darkness beside her.

"I want to live while I'm alive," you whisper.

Then keep me in mind, Buffy, his eyes seem to say. Keep me in mind.

THE END

This is important, but you have to get back to Marcie. If there's any hope of saving her, you have to pick her up and carry her upstairs so you can call 911.

SLAYER ACTION:
Turn to page 64.

So you turn your workout into a little training session—your second since Monday. You do a step routine to much good music. Up and down, up and down, feel the burn . . . while Giles makes little snooty comments about his brains dribbling out of his ears as he reads.

You used to think he was an impossibly stuffy old English guy—until Eyghon showed up (and Ethan Rayne gave you that ugly tatt to lure Eyghon to you). Then you found out that Giles was actually pretty funkadelic back in the sixties. Which would have been cool, if it hadn't involved people dying and Miss Calendar getting possessed. And Angel saving the day by having the demon already inside him duking it out with Eyghon.

Anyway, up and down, up and down, you are feeling pretty good with the ponytail bobbing. . . .

And then Giles says, "When you pulverized the Master's bones, did you destroy his nasal passages?"

You stare at him. "What?" You look around. "Have I somehow entered the mucus dimension?"

SLAYER ACTION:
Turn to page 152.

"**L**et's go check the blood," you say. "How is it *off*? What do you mean?"

"It's . . . it just seems wrong."

"Could you vague that up for me?" Then you make a face—that he can probably see—and say, "Sorry."

"It's all right. I don't know how to explain it. It's nothing I've smelled before."

"Lead on, McAngel," you say, smiling at your own humor. You have the knowledge!

"Okay, we're heading into another tunnel. This is a really twisted set of tunnels." You keep going. There's a rumbling sound, and then the earth shakes. You grab on to Angel and say, "Whoa."

"Earthquake," Angel says grimly.

You also suddenly feel very sad, as if someone had sprayed sorrow all over you. You try to shake out of it. Maybe there's a weird gas down here.

The ground shakes again.

"This tunnel is unstable," Angel says urgently. "We have to get you out of here!"

SLAYER ACTION:
Turn to page 126.

ABOUT THE AUTHOR

Best-selling author **Nancy Holder** has published sixty books and more than two hundred short stories. She has received four Bram Stoker awards for fiction from the Horror Writers Association, and her books have been translated into more than two dozen languages. A graduate of the University of California at San Diego, Nancy is currently a writing teacher at the school. She lives in San Diego with her daughter, Belle, and their growing assortment of pets. Please visit her at www.nancyholder.com.

Buffy lives on . . . in books!

**Stake out a new
Buffy the Vampire Slayer book
every other month!**

"I'm the Slayer. Slay-er. Chosen One? She who hangs out a lot in cemeteries? Ask around. Look it up: 'Slayer *comma* The.'"

—Buffy, "Doomed"

INTO EVERY GENERATION,

A SLAYER IS BORN

Seven years, 144 episodes, three Slayers, two networks, two vampires with souls(!), two Watchers, three principals, two pigs, one Master, one Mayor, countless potentials: It all adds up to one hit show.

The Watcher's Guides, Volumes 1–3, are the *complete* collection of authorized companions to the hit show *Buffy the Vampire Slayer*. Don't be caught dead without them!

Into every generation,
a Slayer is born . . .

Before there was Buffy, there were other Slayers called to protect the world from the undead. Led by their Watchers, they have served as our defense across the globe and throughout history.

In these collections of short stories written by best-selling authors, travel through time to these other Slayers. From France in the fourteenth century to Iowa in the 1980s, the young women have protected the world. Their stories and legacies are unforgettable.

Published by Simon & Schuster

"Witches can't be allowed to alter the fabric of life that way, for selfish reasons. We'd manipulate the world until it came unglued...."
—Tara, "Forever"

In the woods outside Sunnydale, Willow Rosenberg exacted a terrible revenge for the murder of her lover, Tara Maclay: She captured Warren, the murderous leader of the Trio, and flayed him alive. Her best friends, Buffy Summers and Xander Harris, arrived too late to stop her.

But the death of Warren isn't enough for Willow. On the television show, she was brought back to the side of good—but in the new, alternate-reality trilogy, award-winning author Yvonne Navarro asks, What if evil Willow was never stopped?

THE DARKENING

SHATTERED TWILIGHT

BROKEN SUNRISE